Also by Danzy Senna

Symptomatic

Caucasia

Where Did You Sleep Last Night?

Where Did You Sleep Last Night?

A PERSONAL HISTORY

Danzy Senna

Farrar, Straus and Giroux   New York

To Percival

Farrar, Straus and Giroux
18 West 18th Street, New York 10011

Copyright © 2009 by Danzy Senna
Distributed in Canada by Douglas & McIntyre Ltd.
Printed in the United States of America
First edition, 2009

Library of Congress Cataloging-in-Publication Data
Senna, Danzy.
    Where did you sleep last night? : a personal history / Danzy Senna.— 1st ed.
        p.   cm.
    ISBN-13: 978-0-374-28915-7 (hardcover : alk. paper)
    ISBN-10: 0-374-28915-8 (hardcover : alk. paper)
    1. Senna, Danzy.   2. Authors, American—21st century—Biography.   I. Title.

PS3569.E618Z46 2009
813'.54—dc22

                                                                    2008043413

Designed by Abby Kagan

www.fsgbooks.com

10   9   8   7   6   5   4   3   2   1

A thing is mighty big when time and distance cannot shrink it.

—Zora Neale Hurston

Where Did You Sleep Last Night?

1968

In 1975 my mother left my father for the last time. We fled to Guilford, Connecticut. It was a rich town, but we rented an apartment in a tenement that the town's residents referred to only as "the welfare house." The backyard was a heap of dead cars. We lived on the second floor. Below us lived the town's other nonwhite residents, a Korean war bride and her two half-Italian sons. Beside them lived an obese white woman and her teenage son.

I don't know if we were officially hiding out from my father there—or if he knew where we were all that time. In my memory it seems that a long time passed before we saw him again, long enough for me to forget him. And I remember the day he reappeared. I was five, and I heard the doorbell ring. I raced in bare feet to see who was there. I saw, at the bottom of the dimly lit stairwell, a man. His face was hidden in the shadows, but I could make out black curls, light brown skin.

"Hi, baby," he called up to me.

I stared back.

"Don't you know who I am?"

I shook my head.

"You don't know who I am?"

I knew and I didn't know. I had memories of the man at the bottom of the stairwell, both good and bad—but I could not say who he was. I only knew that I had known him, back there in the city, and the sight of him now made me uneasy.

My mother emerged behind me in a housedress. I heard a sound in her throat—a gasp or a sigh—when she saw whom I was talking to.

"See that?" the man shouted up at her. "See what you've done? She doesn't even know who I am. My own child doesn't recognize me."

I began to cry, perhaps recalling now all that we had fled. My mother shushed me. "It's your father," she said, gathering me into her arms. I turned to watch him come toward us up the stairs.

Thirty years later, and he's still asking me that question. "Don't you know who I am?"

There is always that moment—fragile, brief—when I see my father coming toward me from a distance, and I am happy. Particularly in odd places, far from home, like the time he came to visit me at the artists' colony in New Hampshire. I'd been there a few weeks already and had bonded with the other colonists in that fast and furious way friendships can form in isolation. At an artists' colony you live in a bubble, separate from past and present and future. So it felt odd, a little bit intrusive, to have a person from my outside life come visit. But when my father called and asked if he could pop in one afternoon—it was only a few hours' drive from Rhode Island, where he lived—I felt a wave of homesickness and agreed to see him.

I remember sitting and waiting for him in the common room in front of the big picture window surrounded by a crowd of other colonists. It was midday, prime work-time, but as I sat there waiting—and my father was late, very late, as usual—people trickled in one by one, until a small crowd had formed around me. "I hear you're waiting for your father," more than one remarked as they settled onto the couch beside me. And it struck me at some point that they were waiting to see my father too. It was curious to me that they would want to meet him. I wondered why they would not prefer to be working in their cabins, the way they'd come here to do.

As I watched the snow fall slowly outside the window, a thought crept into my mind. I wondered if they were gathered around me out of that old racial curiosity. I thought perhaps they wanted to see if it was true, if somebody who looked so like one of them could really have a black father. It was that old fault line again, and I felt alien from the colonists whom I'd grown to feel were my friends over the past weeks. I felt what I'd felt so many times in my life, that I was a specimen. And I wanted them all to go away so I could wait for my father in private.

And then I saw his blue pickup truck pull up in the driveway outside, and I said, rising, "That's him. He's here." The group around me became quiet, and they all stared out the picture window as he stepped out of his pickup truck in a trench coat, a hat on his head, and made his way across the gravel to the white farmhouse where we waited. I saw him through their eyes, and I felt a surge of pride as I watched him walking through the snow. Pride that he was my father.

My father is handsome—on his good days, even now, when he has not been drinking or eating too much, he is strikingly handsome. A hush fell over the group as they watched him approach. He came through the door, and I felt the eyes of the others on us as I rose to greet him. I hugged him hello, and I remember I made a show of being more affectionate toward him than I would have been if we were unobserved. I felt the need to perform our closeness. In that embrace I wanted to show that I was with him, not them. No matter how friendly I'd been toward them the past few weeks, they did not know the real me.

After the embrace I turned around and introduced him to them, and for a moment everything was perfect. He had not revealed himself. He was just a mysterious, handsome black man in snappy clothes, a mystery man—the paper-doll hero out of a Sidney Poitier movie—who had shown up in New Hampshire to visit his writer daughter. And if I could freeze it there, in that moment of him nodding his head hello, he would be the perfect father—the father of my childhood daydreams. That was what he was to the crowd of white faces who stared at us. I imagined I had gone from being just one of the other colonists to being something far more interesting because of this man by my side.

After they'd all said hello, I shuttled him out the door, saying I wanted to show him my studio. I needed us to disappear quickly before he could do anything to ruin the picture.

Today, in an effort to describe him, I sat down and wrote a list of words—rumors, impressions, lies, truths—that I associate with him.

Intellectual. Alcoholic. Wanderer. Race-man. Con artist. Member, briefly, of the Communist Party. Capitalist. Exile. Chameleon.

A walking, talking contradiction.

He saw people as symbols rather than individuals. Growing up, I could never keep track of which group in the population he mistrusted the most. Whenever I would complain to him about somebody doing something wrong to me—a teacher in school who'd given me a bad grade, a rude sales clerk—he would respond: "What was their last name?" It didn't matter what answer I gave him. Their last name could be anything: Polish, German, Indian, Spanish, Asian, Irish. His response would be the same: a cynical smirk, a shake of the head, as if to say, *Well, what did you expect from one of them?*

He rarely dated black women, but when I walked through Boston with him, he would give the solidarity nod to every black man we passed on the street. For a long time I thought he was a personal friend of every black man in Boston.

His best friend for a time was a paraplegic white lawyer. We'd drive around Boston—the three of us kids crammed in the back with a folded wheelchair—while my father and Shenkman, as my father called him, sat in the front trading get-rich-quick schemes.

I used to daydream about a fantasy father: a cleaned-up version of my own, a father who wore a suit, made money, and didn't get drunk and lose control and who looked just like Billy Dee Williams in the seventies classic *Mahogany*.

My real father was just as handsome but much less smooth, and he seemed to have sprung from nowhere. His mother had died by the time I was three, and his siblings had fled the city and didn't keep in close touch with him or us. I grew up with very little relationship to them. His sister did not want to be mentioned by name in this book, and another sibling asked not to be mentioned at all. The other characters from his youth were still in the Deep South—a place I'd never been. All I had were scraps of information. I knew he'd spent his youth in Alabama and Louisiana. Then, when he was ten, his mother moved north with him and his siblings and settled in Boston's Cabot Street housing projects. There he excelled in his studies and became one in the first cluster of black students to go to Boston University. He married my mother—blue eyes, blue blood—in 1968, only a year after *Loving v. State of Virginia*, the Supreme Court case that overturned the laws banning interracial marriage and only six months after the assassination of Martin Luther King, Jr. By the time my father was twenty-eight, he was the youngest editor at Beacon Press, author of *The Fallacy of IQ,* a seminal book on standardized testing and race, a published poet and short-story writer. He was, in other words, a Negro of exceptional promise. That dangerous phrase—*exceptional promise*—swirled around him as it has swirled around me, like a jinx or a dare.

I looked up these definitions recently in Webster's Dictionary:

Exception: 1) somebody or something that is not included in or does not fit into a general rule, pattern or judgment. 2) The act or condition of being excluded. 3) A clause in a legal document that limits the effect of a part or the whole of it.

Promise: 1) to assure somebody that something will happen or be done; 2) to cause somebody to expect something; 3) an indication that somebody or something will turn out well or successfully.

By the age of thirty, my father had lost everything that mattered to him. Gone was the "Negro of exceptional promise," and in its stead he lived up to all the stereotypes that his fellow Americans had ever secretly or not-so-secretly harbored about black men. He could not consistently stay sober. He got fired from his job. And after my mother left him, he followed her one night to a friend's dinner party and in front of all the guests dragged her down the steps by her hair and beat her in the street.

My mother has, for as long as I can remember, had a slightly crooked nose. It is so subtle you might miss it, this tiny imperfection. As a child, I studied her face closely, traced its lines with my finger, and did notice it—the way her aquiline nose seemed to veer off from its chosen path. Once, I asked her why, and she told me that she broke it when she was a child by opening up the door in a moving car and falling out. She used it as a lesson to me: Never open the door when we're in a moving vehicle. It was the kind of vivid lesson that kids remember. But it wasn't true. My father's fist had made her nose crooked. She is five foot two and he is six foot two, and one time he beat her in an alley in front of two witnesses: a laughing, drunk homeless man who just happened to be there, and my four-year-old brother, who banged on my father's legs with his tiny fists, begging him to stop. She was small but was not one to take it. She left him. He stalked her. In the end she took him to court and got a restraining order against him. He wasn't allowed within one hundred feet of her.

When I was a child, I worried that my mother would die by violent means. I worried she would die by my father's hand. And so it is an odd relief to me to see her growing old now, developing arthritis, the lines spreading across her skin. Aging is pedestrian and gradual, and it is a relief. So many women loathe getting older—they dread their birthdays—but I know, as perhaps all children of violence know, that aging is for the lucky.

Recently I came across an article from the *Boston Sunday Globe* for October 13, 1969, entitled "A Dropout Rejoins the Family of Writers." It is a profile of my mother. At the time she was only a year into her marriage to my father, had just given birth to her first child, and had recently published her first book, a story collection called *Forty Whacks*, named after that old Lizzie Borden playground rhyme.

> Lizzie Borden took an axe
> And gave her mother forty whacks.
> And when she saw what she had done,
> She gave her father forty-one.

The *Globe* article, written by Ellen Goodman, portrays my mother as a rebel who has rejected her aristocratic roots—indeed, has taken that figurative axe to her patrician heritage.

> [Fanny Howe] is the slight and feminine descendant—if not heir—of the Howe family, an impressive lineage of scholars, authors and thoroughly Eminent Bostonians . . . Her grandfather was Mark Anthony De Wolfe Howe, the historian and biographer, known to his Edwardian contemporaries as Mr. Boston. He married Fanny Quincy, of those Quincys . . . Her father was Mark DeWolfe Howe Jr., the biographer of Oliver Wendell Holmes, the Harvard Law School professor and civil rights advocate, who died two years ago. Fanny's mother is the Irish actress and author Mary Manning . . . Of their three daughters Fanny is the second, the rebel, the drop-out, and now, the author.

The article says she is married to "black writer . . . Carl Senna . . . who teaches English and African Literature at Tufts University and is an editor at Beacon Press." The piece is accompanied by a large photograph of my mother holding my four-month-old sister, Ann-Lucien.

At the time of the article my parents lived outside the city, in a town called Marblehead, a protected harbor in Salem Bay. The official website for the town says it is "famous for its unsurpassed contributions to the American Revolution and Civil War." My parents' house overlooked the Atlantic Ocean. Goodman describes my mother standing in the kitchen of that oceanside home unscrewing the top of a jar of peas for her baby daughter, who "kicked her feet impatiently and let out bleeps of hunger sounds." Every detail signifies domestic coziness, the pedestrian normality only underscoring the young family's literary and multiracial exoticism.

Ellen Goodman concludes that "Fanny Howe is a floater, self-contained, in tune with herself if not with conventions. She can unaffectedly meander into a prim author's party with three huge dogs in tow. She belongs to the W. H. Auden poem blown up on her living-room wall, and the Dr. Spock paperback in the nursery. She is concerned, but not overwhelmed by the problems of bringing up the children of their mixed racial marriage."

It is strange—disconcerting even—for me to read the 1969 *Globe* profile of my mother after all that has occurred; to hear Goodman's romantic portrayal of my parents' life together. Even the few mildly complaining details that my mother offers up about my father in the article serve to cast a more romantic light on their union.

"It's hard being married to a writer," she is quoted as saying. "We both experience the same things and it's a question of who will write about them first . . . But the main thing is finding separate places to write in the house."

These are glittery, hopeful people—an interracial couple out of a dream. They are not the same people I met when I came into the world one year later.

The story came to me sideways, the way these things often do. It came to me several years ago, when I was standing on the corner of Brattle Street and Massachusetts Avenue in Harvard Square waiting for the light to change. I looked up and saw what I must have always known but had never really acknowledged: my mother's history—and therefore mine too—was written everywhere. A subway map to Quincy Market. An advertisement for DeWolfe Realtors. Before me was Harvard's campus, where my mother's father and forefathers had studied, taught, and presided. Just a few blocks up was my great-grandfather's ode to tobacco, engraved on a bronze plaque on the wall outside the century-old smoke shop Leavitt and Pierce. It was quite literally all around me: on street signs and statues, on subway maps and plaques.

I had just moved back to the area—my hometown—after twelve years away and was looking at the city for the first time with adult eyes. I'd left the area after high school for college in California and had vowed never to return. However, in the intervening years I'd grown nostalgic for what I'd left, forgetting my original reasons for fleeing, and so now I was back, an adult, lured home by a fancy teaching job.

I saw it that gray winter day in Harvard Square for the first time, really recognized it with a rush of embarrassment, amusement, shame and pride, disgust and glee, all mixed together. Because in the next breath literally I thought of what was not there, the other half of me, my father's side, which I knew nothing about and had never really thought to wonder about until now.

I could go on about my mother's pedigree. Bostonians are

obsessed with pedigrees. They suffer from "grandfather on the brain," as one social critic put it. They make a distinction between long-tailed Bostonians and short-tailed Bostonians. My mother has a long tail—that "impressive lineage of scholars, authors and thoroughly Eminent Bostonians" mentioned in the *Sunday Globe* article. She can trace her lineage back to the *Mayflower*. The Quincys. The Adamses. The Huntingtons. The Howes. The DeWolfs, as they once used to spell their name. Her history is woven into the myth of the city itself.

One day I spent an hour in the Berg Collection of the New York Public Library looking at a signed first edition of *The Gentle Americans: Biography of a Breed*, written by my mother's aunt, Helen Huntington Howe, and published in 1965. It describes the world of my great-grandfather, Mark Anthony DeWolfe Howe, essayist, biographer, and editor of *The Atlantic Monthly*.

The librarian in the Berg Collection was very careful when putting *The Gentle Americans* in front of me. She placed first a velvet cloth on the table, then two foam cradles to protect the spine from bending, then a strand of what looked like prayer beads to weigh the pages down, and then, and only then, did she lay the book down for me to open. The book is described on the dust jacket as "A delightful re-creation of the literary and social life of some remarkable Bostonians." Remarkable indeed.

One notable ancestor, Captain "Nor'west" James DeWolf, is described as having a record that is "the most appalling and therefore the most successful [of all the Bristol slave-runners] . . . the old trader . . . sometimes had to put down his morning cup of coffee because he seemed to see blood on the surface of it, and when he saw it he remembered his throwing a slave with smallpox out of a boat, and chopping off his hands with an axe when he tried to pull himself back over the gunwale."

For many generations the gentle Americans whom Helen Howe celebrates in her family memoir tried to downplay their ancestral connection to the slave trade.

My great-great-grandfather on my mother's side, another Mark Anthony DeWolfe Howe, was the first Episcopal bishop of Pennsylvania. It was "the Bishop," as he was known, who in his generation added the final "e" to the Wolf family name . . . to add "tone." He was the husband of three wives and the father of eighteen children—a figure whom his son, my great-grandfather, found "rather mortifying."

The Bishop also, in regard to his more unseemly family history, had a special way of mincing words.

"In one way or another, some of our people," he wrote in a private family history printed for his children, "had plantations in the West Indies [and] there came to be a considerable colored population, and I recollect that for a while in my early days they occupied a certain part of town called Goree."

He was, of course—in his own oblique way—referring to Goree Island off the West Coast of Africa, where this "considerable colored population" were stored before they were shipped off, stacked in chains, below deck.

My great-grandfather, being a liberal Bostonian man of letters, was more honest about the source of his ancestors' infamy. But, being a liberal Bostonian man of letters, he didn't like to dwell on the topic, found it disturbing or embarrassing, and was "considerably saddened" when one of his more rebellious nephews, George Howe, published his scathing account of the family's involvement in the slave trade, *Mount Hope*. "I tried to offer [Father] the bleak comfort of suggesting that many other New England families had been pretty bad too," writes Helen Howe in *The Gentle Americans*. " 'I'm afraid not as bad as ours,' was his answer."

Nevertheless *The Gentle Americans* is for the most part celebratory of what Helen Howe calls "ideal exemplars of a breed that is now extinct." Included in three generations of my family tree are "three mayors of Boston, two hosts of Lafayette, one Harvard president."

White noise, in the Random House Dictionary, is defined as "a steady unvarying, unobtrusive sound, as an electronically produced drone or the sound of rain, used to make or obliterate unwanted sounds." White noise is the sound you hear but don't know you are hearing. It is the sound that puts you to sleep.

That day I could hear white noise in the shush of tires on wet gravel, the whisper of northeastern arrogance, the drone of a history lesson of inherited accomplishment, privilege passed down through the ages. And seeing these signs of the written half everywhere, it was the absent story that I hungered to find—that is, my father's family story, and through it to find my father himself, he who seemed to have had no tail, or tale, at all.

Though I grew up with my father, I knew only random details about his past. There were black relatives in the South we didn't see, who called occasionally and asked after the "little white children," as they called us in a not-so-subtle disownment. My father's full name is Carl Francisco José Senna. He grew up not knowing his father, the source of his Spanish middle name, aware of only what his mother told him: he was the son of a Mexican boxer who had abandoned his wife with three kids and was never seen again. I knew my father had feelings about the past, that he had loved his mother, and that the

people he grew up with in the South were important to him because he had named my sister and me after them. But the stories
of his childhood were not really stories, just odd, incongruent
details that slipped into conversation, it seemed, by accident.
There was no black extended family, ever, and no mythology of
his people engraved in stone to remind us of their importance.

As my father says, one side is unusually—even compul-
sively—documented, and the other is a black hole that, when
you call into it—*Who are you?*—only swallows the very
question.

Today I live in southern California, where these histories—both
my mother's and my father's—make no sense. New money, new
malls, new races—they crop up every day in this land of perpetual amnesia. I am nine months pregnant. I have left behind my
first family and am on to creating my second, chosen family,
and so in a sense I am free of all this history.

My husband and I live in a fancy brand-new apartment
building where television studios house actors and talent show
contestants each year. Wannabe movie stars pass me in the hall
on my way to the trash chute. My husband and I have noticed
there are a large number of attractive interracial couples and
their café-au-lait progeny living in the building. We had not
sought out racial comfort when we were looking for a place to
live—just ease and sunlight and high ceilings and a neighborhood where we could walk. But what we've stumbled on is
something I could not have imagined existed, growing up in the
rigidly stratified world of Boston. What we have now is multi-
cultural to the point of absurdity. The week we moved in, our
neighbors from down the hall—a white fashion model and

her television personality husband, a first-generation Nigerian American—left us a gift on our doorstep, a pair of tiny, baby-size fur boots, in preparation for our baby's arrival. The Indian woman in the lobby gave me the name of her pediatrician. The very trim and pretty building manager, a black woman named Laine, mentioned a Mexican nanny she could recommend. There is so much approval and friendly anticipation of our baby before he is even born that I begin to fantasize this is a secret cult, like the one in the apartment building in *Rosemary's Baby*, except that this group is based not on devil worship but on miscegenation worship. It strikes me that my husband and I are only passing as an interracial couple. I wonder if these same people will be disappointed when they find out, if they find out, that we are in actuality something far more old-fashioned—a redbone black man with a high yellow woman—that our backgrounds are embarrassingly similar, a swirl of slave masters and slaves.

Outside the window of my office where I sit writing about the tangled past are palm trees and cars zipping past on Rossmore Avenue, and across the street is the Country Club Manor, an elegant old building where a famous comedian is rumored to keep his pied-à-terre. Farther down the block is the Mauretania, an art deco building commissioned by Jack Haley, the actor who played the Tin Man in *The Wizard of Oz*. Two doors down sits the Ravenswood, a building Mae West lived in until her death.

I suppose it is no coincidence that it is here I have chosen to give birth, so far from Boston and my history, far from my parents' saga of the Deep South and the Deep North. Here, in the pale light of my chosen amnesia, I can imagine I am free.

I had a nightmare when I was eight years old, so graphic and brutal I remember it even today. In it my mother opened the door to her bedroom and walked toward me, weeping. In the place where one of her breasts should have been was a bloody, gaping hole. Nothing is lost on children.

One of my mother's oldest friends said to me once of my parents' split: "It was the ugliest divorce in Boston's history." Surely there were worse, but I knew just what he meant. The divorce was so ugly because the marriage was so unequivocally beautiful. My parents' marriage had been steeped from the start in symbolism. Together they were going to snub the history that divided them and create an ahistorical utopia in our home. When their marriage failed so drastically—when history seemed to catch up with them—it must have seemed to them and those who witnessed that rupture like the death of a promise far larger than their wedding vows.

In the years that followed, my father continued his downward course. He didn't pay child support. When we begged him for money, he would shrug and say, "I don't have any. You can't squeeze water out of a rock." He could barely support himself. He would disappear for weeks on end. He was allowed to see us kids, but only if there was a court-approved chaperone present. He wasn't allowed to enter our house. He would beep outside when he came to pick us up.

I loathed him, feared him, and yet loved him. I remember one night, my tenth birthday, my mother's relatives were gathered in our kitchen for a party. Weeks earlier my father had asked me what I wanted for a present, and I'd said a desk. I had said it just to say something, certain I would get no such thing. But that night, as we were serving the cake, I heard it: his signature beeping outside. I tore down the stairs with my sister.

There he was, unloading a giant white box from the back of his car. It was my present, a desk—assembly required, but a desk nonetheless. He'd bought it at Woolworth's. The price tag was only half torn off. After he drove away, my sister and I lugged the box inside. I sat down to open it on the kitchen floor, with my mother and her relatives gathered around me, their arms crossed, dubious frowns on their faces. Inside were plywood planks and a slab of pine that was the desktop, a Baggie of nails and screws, and an instruction manual written in English on one side, Taiwanese on the other. For the next twenty minutes, one of my visiting white relatives set about to try to assemble the desk, but the directions were impossible, and even when she figured them out, she couldn't get the desk to come together. Eventually she gave up, leaving the wood in a pile on the floor. "It's a piece of junk," I remember her saying. "Cheap bastard." Everybody agreed. The desk was worse than cheap. It was defective. While they went back to the table for cake, I disappeared into my bedroom. My sister found me there a few minutes later. She didn't ask why I was crying. She understood how badly I'd wanted that desk to come together, and so she just held me, quietly, in the dark.

There were good moments with my father, but many more bad ones. Police and court injunctions. Lies and humiliations. Too many afternoons waiting for him on the sidewalk outside our house hours after he'd said he would be there. The summer of my sister's twelfth birthday, we planned a party at my father's apartment. He seemed to be changing for the better. He had a new job and had gone a month without a drink. Besides, there were practical reasons: his apartment was near our school, and our friends could walk there after classes. My sister and I arrived at his place at three o'clock with our gang of friends, each girl carrying a bag of party preparations. I knew something was wrong before we even opened the door. I could hear Barry White on the record player, that seventies nostalgia always a bad sign. Inside, my father was an unshaven mess, still in his pajamas, slurring, barely able to stand on his feet. He stank of vodka. My sister, always a quick thinker, told the girls that our father had a health condition and that it was the medication that made him act funny. We'd have to go out for pizza on the corner instead. The girls exchanged confused looks, but nobody stated the obvious. My sister and I kept up a cheery facade but rode home that evening with our mother in stony silence.

Over time I stopped asking my father for birthday presents. I stopped running down the stairs, two steps at a time, when I heard him beeping outside. Instead, I would approach his car slowly, hands shoved in my pockets, body half turned away.

Once, when I was eight or nine, long after their separation, I asked my mother if she had ever loved my father.

She looked off into the distance and pondered the question for a moment.

"It was something else," she said, still looking off, as if speaking to herself. "Not love. Something else."

Then she kissed me good night and left the room.

After their physical contact had ceased, my siblings and I were left with the sound of their fighting. My mother never censored her negative thoughts about my father, daily hissed curses about him over some failure or another. Her slew of complaints about him was never-ending. When complaining about each other to us kids, she referred to him as "your father" and he to her as "your mother" so that we children became owners of the problem. She often sent us kids out to his car with orders to ask him for money, for despite her pedigree, she had no inheritance.

And of course we also, regularly, heard the anger articulated in my father's tirades, on the phone to her or in messages he would convey to us to give to her. Whatever the form, it was endless verbal warfare, back and forth or through us, the conduits.

For many years, at night, just as I was trying to fall asleep, their fighting voices would continue in my head. It always went the same way: I would hear their imaginary voices quarreling back and forth, at first just a whisper in my ear that would speak progressively louder and faster until they melted together like those tigers chasing each other around the tree in *Little Black Sambo*. They became in my head an enraged yellow blur of anger, and I could not distinguish one from the other.

And then there were the interrogations—my father's suspicious questioning of us kids about my mother's whereabouts, her private life. At some point after the divorce my mother started seeing a new man. He lived out of town but came often to visit for weekends; other weekends we went to visit him. My mother was still afraid of my father and made us three kids swear not to tell him about her new relationship. I was eight, my sister was nine, my brother was six. My father found out about it somehow anyway, and on custody visits with him he began to grill us about the new man. My brother, the youngest, had bonded the most strongly with my mother's new boyfriend and, being just a small child, was most vulnerable to these inquisitions. While my sister and I were old enough to carefully shake our heads and lie during my father's questions, I remember once, during one of these inquisitions—we were at a local pizza joint called The Same Old Place—my brother slipped up and called my father by the other man's name by mistake.

My father whipped around. "What did he just call me? What name did he just call me?" he demanded.

My brother's lower lip trembled in fear.

I heaped abuse on my six-year-old little brother, telling him he was an idiot for saying that, so stupid for slipping up, how could he have been so stupid?

In the absence of a context for my father, a black extended family and history, I am left with only random details about my father himself, the ones that exist in fragments, devoid of plot:

The dog that appeared in his apartment one day—he named it Wolfgang—a Doberman puppy that pissed on my shoe when I took it out for a walk. My father gave Wolfgang away. He could not care for himself, he could not care for us, he could care even less for a four-legged dependent.

The collection of ghetto pulp on his bookshelf by authors Iceberg Slim and Donald Goines. Me, in puberty, sneaking peeks at the books, becoming aroused by the scenes of the prostitutes getting raped by the pimp. Him finding the book in our room and demanding to know who had been reading it. Me, face burning, pretending I did not know. Him, out of kindness perhaps, pretending to believe me.

The way whenever I would mention a new friend at school, his first question was "Who is she?" I always knew what he meant. *What is she?* Meaning, *Black or white?*

My first Halloween in Brookline, attending the school near his house. It was my new schoolmates who left the bananas on my father's porch. They did not know the black man who had just moved in there was my father. They did not know I was black, and they did not believe me when I told them.

Coming into his apartment one day to find stacks of one-hundred-dollar bills lined up on the living room floor. Around it were copies of a newspaper he'd somehow gotten off the ground: *The Real News*. By the following week he was somehow broke again.

Wednesdays and Sundays. Our designated days with Papa. He would bring us to movies that were often decidedly not appropriate for children. *Quest for Fire*, in which, at eleven, I saw cave people having sex, doggie style. *The Godsend*, a British horror movie about a little blond girl adopted into a family at birth, who kills each of the biological children one by one in lethal sibling rage. I could not sleep for weeks.

The way he took so unbearably long to pick his order from the menu in restaurants, and would change his mind five times before the waiter left our table.

The way he sat hunched over, his eyes fixed on a spot above my head, as he ate without joy or pause.

The voice game. It wasn't really a game, because a game is fun, a game you play voluntarily. But it had the trappings of a game in that we played it to solve the puzzle that could not be solved, the puzzle of his voice. He would call, and I would listen to him speak on the other end of the line and try to tell if he was drunk or not. Often it was obvious—he was slurring and nonsensical. But other times it was more subtle—he was only on his way to getting drunk, or he was in the aftermath of the night before. "What's wrong with your voice?" we would each ask our father. "Why do you sound so funny?" He had several stock lies. He had eaten bad Chinese food and had been throwing up for days. He was on medication for his asthma that made him talk funny.

Flashdance. The movie had just come out in theaters. My sister and I had been looking forward to it all week, and he was unusually prompt, beeped outside at the appointed time, and we went running to his car, giving our mother brusque kisses at the door, pulling our brother along behind us. My father was in good spirits as we got in the car and started the engine. But something happened to me. I was suddenly gripped by an intense feeling of separation anxiety from my mother—a sense that she was being left out of the fun and that she would be lonely at home without us. I couldn't leave. My father and my siblings were baffled: the evening I'd been looking forward to was happening, and now I wanted to get out of the car and go inside and spend the evening at home alone with my mother. I grew hysterical when they tried to convince me to come, so my father finally let me out of the car and, shrugging, said he was sorry I wasn't joining them. I stood on the curb, watching them drive off to the movie, already half-regretting my decision.

And the fact was, as soon as I got inside I understood that my mother was fine without us—was in fact enjoying a much-needed evening at home alone, and she seemed irritated that I'd decided to come back and spend the evening with her. But by then it was too late to change my mind. I'd taken to heart—the way children do—so much of their careless warring rhetoric. I'd believed everything they said about each other in our presence, and I believed that to enjoy my father, to love my father, to accept the fact that despite everything he could be fun, would be to betray my mother. I spent the evening in sullen remorse and was nearly in tears when my sister came bounding through my bedroom door hours later to tell me how *amazing* the movie had been. And guess what? Jennifer Beals was black like us, *just like us.* I should have seen it.

I remember him accomplishing certain fatherly tasks, like flying out to my college graduation in California, but then in my dorm room, immediately following the ceremony, asking me if he could borrow money. He just needed twenty dollars to get back to the airport.

The snapping sensation in my brain when I was angry with him.

My mother, trying to downplay the extent of the damage, to rewrite the narrative somehow so it seemed less awful, made this strange comment to me from time to time: "You never had a father. He was more of a big brother to you." Me one day correcting her: "No, Mummy, everyone has a father. He was the father I got."

Him calling our house one day when I was thirteen, telling each of us kids, one by one, that he was an alcoholic and that he was sorry for the way he'd hurt us and that he loved us. His voice sounded strange. But this time he was not sick and he was not drunk. He was weeping. Me thinking that everything was going to be different now, that he was going to become strong and sober and debonair, he was going to be the father I'd been waiting for.

I had a moment of confusion recently when looking at my parents' marriage certificate. In both the groom and the bride sections, the third piece of information requested after name and age is "Color." While my mother is listed as "white," my father is listed as "brown" rather than "black" or "negro." Apparently my father insisted on this term. He was trying to make a point about race as a social construct rather than an essential biological category. If they wanted to know his color, he would give them the literal color of his skin. He wanted to call attention to the absurdity of racial categorization, even on this most personal of documents.

Looking at the form now, the word *brown* seems to point as well to the murkiness of my father's origins.

He was born in the small bayou town of Jennings, Louisiana, in 1944. The Jim Crow South was alive and well. Miscegenation was a crime punishable by imprisonment and, more often, lynching—though in Louisiana the races had been mixing for a long time. My father's own father was not present for the birth. Instead a large family of Creoles, so light they could "pass," surrounded my grandmother. Their relationship to my father's unequivocally dark-skinned mother—how she ended up in their home—was not clear to my father. They were the first of many surrogate families—people whose relationship to him and his siblings and his mother that he could not, at the time nor in retrospect, define—strangers he would be taken in by and raised by along the way.

Of his father, all he has is a newspaper clipping of the boxer Francisco Jose Senna, but no memories of the man himself.

My father's mother, Anna, lived with us when I was small. We all called her Nana, to distinguish her, I suppose, from our Irish grandmother, whom we called Grandma. *Nana* is, I notice only now, an anagram for her first name, Anna. An anagram is, of course, a scrambling of letters, and it seems now, after all I have learned, that Nana was a disguise Anna wore, a scrambling of signifiers that kept her safe from detection.

I remember scattered details about her—the simple blue cotton dress she wore around the house, the Wrigley's spearmint gum she gave to my sister and me every day when she got home from work. In pictures she is a sloe-eyed, brown-skinned woman who is rarely looking directly at the camera. Her shyness, a discomfort with being looked at or paid too much attention to, is apparent even in pictures. She is always looking down, away, or standing off in the background, like a marginal note at the edge of a text.

According to my parents, I resemble Anna the most of their three children. Though I am fairly tall and she was short, though I am light and she was dark, we share physical traits; the same gap in our teeth, the same long arms and broad shoulders, the same delicate fingers and flat feet. I inherited her bad eyesight. Once, in high school, when I approached my father's car, he looked up and blinked at me, slightly startled.

"You look like my mother," he said. I remember feeling pleased.

Anna was polite to the point of meekness. She lived in the projects in Boston with her three light-skinned children. Her best friend at work, a gay white man named Jackie whom she ate lunch with every day, wept during her funeral service. Apparently I did too.

Because the memories I have of her and the stories my parents have passed down about her are both so few, they have become the whole picture, exaggerated in their significance.

One winter night Anna was babysitting for my sister and me while my parents went out to dinner. When they came home, they found her shivering outside in the doorway to our house, wearing only her thin cotton housedress and slippers. She'd gone outside for a moment to get a piece of wood for the fire, and the door had locked behind her. For hours Anna stood at the window, shivering, numb, watching my sister and me—two and one years old—playing in the living room with no adult supervision except for her, the invisible woman standing helplessly outside in the snow. She'd been too shy to go ask the neighbors for help, so she stood instead for hours freezing in the cold. She'd perhaps felt like too much of an outsider in the northern urban landscape. Whatever the case, it was soon after that night that she came down with pneumonia, and the lung cancer that had been in remission resurfaced and killed her.

She was a devout Catholic who went to church every day.

She was the darkest-skinned person in our house. She was the source of color—the otherness—that would be watered down with the two subsequent generations. Her children were lighter than she was, and her grandchildren were lighter still.

I was nearly what they call an "Irish twin"—only fourteen months younger than my sister, Ann-Lucien—and my mother had her hands full with her firstborn and a rocky marriage when I was born. Anna picked up the slack, that is, the new baby, me. In so many of the photos from that time I am in Anna's arms and my sister is in my mother's arms. When Anna died, I was two. We held a wake at our big old house, and I tottered amid the guests calling, "Nana!" What I remember of her now is not much. She was only fifty-two when she died. A lifetime of cigarettes and bad diet and perhaps despair had morphed into a malignant mass first in her lungs, later in her breast.

As far as I knew, it was with Anna that my father's history began and ended. He had no past that we knew of beyond her. He had Southern relatives—or were they family friends? I wasn't sure. My father's connection to the South, a place I'd never been, showed up only in occasional stories he told when we were kids. The jagged scar running across his upper lip was the result of his childhood love of figs. He'd climbed high into a fig tree trying to pick one of those delectably sweet fruits, and before he could reach it, he fell, splitting open his mouth. He named my sister and me after Southern relatives, aunts we never knew whom he felt the need to honor. Of my namesake, Emma Danzy, I had only a few details to paint a portrait, details I found romantic as a child: Emma Danzy was stone blind and had long straight black hair and Indian blood. In the absence of real, living breathing relatives, these shards of information were all we had of my father's past.

To those who thought to wonder about Anna's story, there were gaps—places where the portrait did not come together. She worked as a lowly clerk, but was clearly more educated than her white Irish coworkers. She read Dostoyevsky and Chekhov, and was reading Solzhenitsyn's *The Gulag Archipelago* the summer before she died. She loved opera and classical music and jazz. (She made an impression on my mother's Wasp family. Long after her death, they would describe her to me as "dignified" and "articulate"—words I came to associate, at an early age, with a kind of coded liberal racism.) Anna would admit, if pushed, that she had not one but two college degrees. She got her bachelor's degree from Alabama State College and her master's in music and teaching from Xavier College in New Orleans. She was, by all accounts, a musical prodigy—and at Alabama State proved herself to be a gifted jazz pianist who played with Erskine Hawkins's famous swing band.

Yet in Boston, my mother says Anna refused to so much as put her hands on the keys of our family piano.

So there were at least two versions of her: Nana, the small, silent woman in a housedress who shuffled around the house, cleaning and caring for children, saying her prayers and bothering no one—and Anna, the one who emerged in fragments of a story, an ambitious and educated black woman, who had been a bon vivant of the Louisiana jazz world of the thirties and forties and who had left all she knew in the South at some point and never looked back.

Even to her children there were pieces of Anna's story that did not make sense. How to explain the color difference? She was a deep dark brown verging on black—yet her children were the light copper color of pennies. My father had soft black curls. All of their features spoke of a heritage lighter, whiter than their mother's—my father's thin lips, his sister's light-colored eyes.

Anna's explanation: Their father was a "white Mexican." She said she'd met Francisco José Senna one night while playing in a jazz club in Harlem. He was a friend and trainer of boxing greats Jersey Joe Walcott and Sugar Ray Robinson, she said, and through their association frequented the black nightclub scene. After they got married, she said, he became a drunk and abused her before eventually abandoning her.

All that my father has as evidence of his father's existence is a newspaper clipping, a short profile written about Francisco by a sports columnist at the Reading, Pennsylvania, *Eagle*. The headline reads: MEXICAN FIGHTER CAMPS IN READING AND MAY MAKE THIS HIS HOME BASE. Next to the article is the faded photograph of a pugilist thug, a nose clearly broken and reset many times, close-set eyes and high cheekbones, a defiant expression.

The article is by a sportswriter named Bill Reedy, whose photo also sits at the top of the page, a thin bespectacled white man who writes in jaunty sports-page fragments. The text is peppered with ellipses used not to imply the omission of words but rather to give the piece the immediacy of a news report just off the wires.

The Cisco Kid is in town, maybe to stay . . . That's the fighting name of Francisco Senna, who came out of his native Mexico in quest of ring fame in this country and has waged some very important bouts . . . He is without a manager at the present time and is ready and willing to locate in Reading on a permanent basis if the right man comes along to handle his fistic affairs . . . He intends to start training daily . . . He's living at the Hotel Milner and ready to talk business . . . educated in San Antonio, Tex. . . . He was just getting somewhere when prematurely matched with Henry Armstrong in Havana, Cuba . . . He was knocked out in the second round in that bout . . . Since that engagement, he has lost only seven con-

tests, one on a decision to Cecil Hudson on the West Coast . . .
He has helped train Sugar Ray Robinson and Beau Jack for
championship contests . . . This widely-traveled leather pusher,
who weighs between 140 and 155 pounds, spent nine months
in the United States Army and was on special assignment
boxing for the soldiers and instructing them on the use of
gloves . . . He is only 26 years old.

These sparse—and I suspect inflated—details of Francisco's
life are all we know of the man, so he became over the years a
character out of a novel for each of us. We clung to the few details we gleaned from the throwaway article, repeated them
when necessary, to explain our name, to explain our features,
and it was the very lack of information that allowed Francisco
to become a man of myth—a GI Joe character come to life, a
masculine romantic archetype with exotic heritage. He became
the detail I enjoyed repeating when asked about my background. "My grandfather was a Mexican boxer," I would say.
"He fought Henry Armstrong in Cuba. He got knocked out in
the first round." Even his failures created the substance of
pride.

Beyond these details, my father could never get any real information about Francisco out of Anna. He and his siblings just
accepted what she told them: that she'd had three children by
the man, who then disappeared, probably back over the border
after President Eisenhower's "Operation Wetback" of the fifties.
It strikes me only now as odd that she had three children by this
character, and none of the children remembers ever having laid
eyes on him. It was as if she had been impregnated three times
by a ghost. But growing up, I accepted the story because it was
the only one we had.

Still, strange cracks in the official story of my father and his siblings' origins emerged over the years.

When my parents got married, my father ordered his baptismal certificate from the Catholic Church. He had never seen it before, and what came in the mail was confusing, a document with strangely mangled information on each line. On the line for NAME is not the name my father had grown up using, the homage to his mysterious Mexican father—Carl Francisco José Senna—but rather a stranger's name: "Carl Francis Franklyn."

Franklin was Anna's maiden name, but here it is spelled with a *y* and not an *i*, as if she were already beginning the process of distancing herself from the facts.

On the next line, under FATHER, he found not Francisco, the Mexican boxer of fairy tale and myth, but instead somebody by the name of Carl Franklyn.

At the bottom of the form, the signature of the priest performing the baptism reads: "Father Francis E. Ryan."

Today I wrote down all of these names and looked at them on a piece of paper, as if the sight of them would trigger a revelation as to what they all mean.

Carl *Francis* Franklyn.

Carl *Franklyn*.

Anna *Franklin*.

Francisco Senna.

Father Francis E. Ryan.

All lined up, they look like a puzzle—the odd echoes in each name of the one before it. Names, as well as official documents, become here an occasion to deceive, bury, obfuscate. Only questions swim up to me. Why did Anna use a false name—Carl Franklyn—when listing my father's father? Why did she misspell her maiden name as Franklyn? Why is my father given the middle name Francis rather than Francisco on this form? Is it possible he was named for Francis the priest, who signed the form, and not for the Mexican boxer?

The baptismal certificates of the subsequent two siblings—born over the next three years, straighten the paternity story out in stages, as if the author—Anna—were clearing her throat, concocting the lies as she told them. One is listed as the child of a father called Francis J. Senna; a girl is listed as the child of a father named, finally, Francisco Senna.

After Anna died, there was nobody else to connect us to my father's past. His siblings scattered to the wind, it seemed, never to be seen again, and there was just him, the only black man in the room who seemed to have sprung from nowhere, weaned on white liberal hopes and social uplift policies, that perpetual *Guess Who's Coming to Dinner* guest, young, gifted, and black, with a blue-eyed, blond-haired white woman on his arm.

In place of a flesh-and-blood black family, in place of black roots, in place of a coherent black community with a history we could touch or feel, he grew obsessed with the idea of blackness, the idea of race, and how to hammer racial consciousness home to his three light-skinned children.

He projected his own sense of isolation and fear of extinction onto us, his children.

When our friends were white, he blamed my mother for our lack of black friends. He insisted she bring us to an after-school program in Roxbury for black youth, where my sister and I were outcasts. It was my mother's job to drop us off and pick us up—to do the grunt work of his racial bidding.

My father constructed for himself—and imposed on us—a blackness that was intellectual and defensive, abstract and negatively defined (always in relation to whiteness). And it worked: My siblings and I never once felt ourselves to be anything but black. We became comfortable in all-black worlds while he remained isolated, forever a token. He had strayed so far from blackness that he himself could never go home. He did not talk about his childhood. He did not talk about his past or his mother's past. Instead he talked incessantly and abstractly about black suffering and racial inequality, but he did not talk about his personal tale of suffering, the particular story that was at the heart of everything. Did he not feel his own story was important enough? Did he believe it had to be transmuted into the symbolic and historical? It had to become a story of black suffering in the abstract because the individual story was too difficult to bear.

More fragments:

The eczema patches on the skin of his fingers that felt like leather. (Later these same patches emerged on my own fingers, and I felt an odd relief in this connection, as if I'd needed proof that I was his daughter.)

The two-tone color of his upper lip: one half pale, the other dark, as if this lip belonged to two different men, not one.

The photo of Francisco, the man he believes to be his father, shows the same two-toned lip. There is no body to exhume. No DNA to recover. So this image, the resemblance we find in this fading newsprint face, is the only evidence we have that this man is his father.

The smell of his Cypress Street apartment: sweet and musty, a smell I associate with loneliness. It was a tenement in Brookline, Massachusetts, on the edge of Whiskey Point, surrounded by Irish American working-class racists, the same ones who left bananas on his porch his first Halloween there and who later spray-painted a misspelled epithet NIGERS GO HOME on the wall of the playground next to his house.

The office—a pile of unpaid bills and half-finished manuscripts amid boxes of those bright yellow-and-black booklets, Cliffs Notes, which he had penned for quick cash: *Alice in Wonderland, Black Boy, One Hundred Years of Solitude.* He wrote study guides of the greats for generations of student cheats to come.

The metal change basket on the desk in his office was filled mostly with pennies. He didn't pay regular child support, but we were allowed to dig through the basket after school and spend any silver we found on junk food at Kirkman's, the Armenian grocery on the corner.

One of my father's girlfriends, a thin white woman. I remember her long pale face and the round glasses she wore that deflected but didn't hide the glint of mental illness in her eyes. Once for Father's Day I gave my father a painting I'd done in my fifth-grade art class. I don't remember what the painting portrayed, only that he hung it up on the wall of his apartment.

The next week, when I returned to his house after school, I saw it still hung there, but it was different, more ragged somehow. When I looked closely, I saw that it had been torn down and crumpled up and then flattened out and hung back up. And when I looked even more closely, I saw there were fingernail scratches on the surface, making ridges in the paint. When I asked my father what happened, he said his girlfriend did it. "She's jealous," he said. I nodded as if I understood.

The time when I was eleven and found a giant rat floating in the toilet of my mother's home. I was at the house alone and, hysterical, I called my mother at work. Without missing a beat, she told me to call my father and get him to come over. I remember being surprised; this was after she'd spent months fighting to acquire a restraining order keeping him away from her and her property. But I did what she said and he rushed over, fished the swollen rat out, then obediently left.

The way he kept the receipts for birthday gifts he gave to us. In case my mother brought him to court to demand back child-support payments, he could show these birthday gift receipts to the judge as proof that he was indeed contributing.

His fixation on my sister. The oldest, his chosen one, she was treated by him less as a favorite child than as an only child. She sat beside him in that passenger seat of his car, bearing the full weight of his influence. She was our buffer zone. She soaked up the teachings he espoused so that by the time they reached my brother and me in the backseat, they were weaker in their influence—just a vapor. (In photos of her even as a young child, I see beneath her high forehead her already worried, too adult eyes, like black pinpricks, staring back at the photographer.)

One of my earliest memories: him coming home drunk and pulling my mother out of bed. We children—three hot bodies—had been sleeping with her. My sister and I crept out of bed and followed them down to the living room, where I recall a sense of menace, sounds of fighting, impending violence, my mother's cries. My sister led me to the kitchen. There she climbed up on a stool beside the telephone. There was a number beside the phone—the number of our neighbor under the words IN CASE OF EMERGENCY. She was a registered nurse, and her children were our age and we played with them often. My sister, four years old, called this neighbor. She told the woman that our little baby brother was choking on a penny and asked if she could come over. The woman knew that this was a lie, knew it was a kind of child code, and came anyway, to my mother's rescue, and interrupted whatever was about to take place.

His jokes, relentless, repetitive, mean, often very funny. How the butt of his jokes was so often other, more successful black male writers: a self-satisfied legal scholar in Cambridge, an obese playwright in Roxbury. Once we saw the obese playwright while we idled in my father's car at a stoplight on Blue Hill Avenue. My father—still thin—pointed at the man and said, "Stick a pin in that fool's neck, and gravy'll come out."

The way he was perpetually late—late in a way that I have never seen anybody be late before or since. If he told us he was coming to pick us up at five, he would not arrive until eight, more likely nine. It was a reliable, extreme lateness—a compulsion to be late, an aversion to being on time. There are too many times to count, all those days spent waiting on street corners in the orange twilight, our bags packed for our overnight with him. Losing hope, going inside, watching television with our coats on for a while, eventually getting too hot in our coats and taking them off, but not putting them away, starting to play together, but knowing even as we settled into the evening—in the comfort of our mother's home—that he could show up at any moment, so we should not get too comfortable, should not make ourselves too at home where we were. And sure enough, in the darkness, as we three kids were getting tired before the flickering television, there it would be, the familiar horn beeping outside. And my brother, my sister, and I would rise and put back on our coats and trudge out with our bags to meet his car where it shone, dark chrome in the darkness, yellow headlights blazing, one hundred feet away.

Today I sat down and looked at the saddest of the files I have gathered, read them alone in the quiet and privacy of my slate gray office. The lives described in the documents seem as far away from the world I inhabit today as indeed they are. They are documents I received last year from the Bureau of Catholic Charities, describing the Zimmer Home, otherwise known as "The Infant of Prague Memorial Home." Included in the packet I received from the church are photographs of the Zimmer Home, washed-out color pictures from the late fifties and early sixties showing black children, the orphans, scattered across a lawn playing kick ball.

This was one of the many "homes" my father inhabited as a child. His mother, Anna, disappeared for great portions of his childhood. He was left in one temporary home after another throughout the South, sometimes in the care of Anna's friends and family members, other times in the care of Catholic institutions. The worst of them was the Zimmer Home. Anna left him and his siblings there when he was five, purportedly so she could pursue her education.

"That's where I got so fucked-up," was all my father would say of the experience.

Through the Catholic charities, I was able to get in touch with another former resident of the Zimmer Home who was more descriptive about his experience at the orphanage. He is a black man just slightly younger than my father, and asked that he not be named in the book. I will call him J. He told me when we spoke on the phone that things had happened to him in the Zimmer Home that he'd only ever been able to confide to his wife. He said the Zimmer Home was a "horror story."

There were beatings. The children were called every name in the book. And there was sexual abuse by the nuns.

"It happened to me there," J told me. "That's soul theft." Then he went silent. I could hear through the phone that he was crying at the memory of what had occurred there.

Both my father and J describe a place where the white nuns swore like sailors and called the children in their care "dirty niggers."

The Zimmer Home was started with the noblest of stated intentions, founded by Rev. Henry Zimmer of Brooklyn, New York, who, while touring Mobile, Alabama, "felt the need for a home for the neglected, orphaned and dependent Negro children." He donated $5,000 for the purchase of a run-down frame building in a town on the outskirts of Mobile known as Prichard. The home's aim was to "care for poor, unfortunate colored boys and girls between the ages of three and sixteen, regardless of religious denomination."

Overcrowded, the school was run by nuns from Poland and Ireland, who also taught at the nearby St. James Major Parochial School operated by Josephite priests. While two sisters remained at home each day to care for the preschool children, four sisters trudged up the muddy road to the school, four or five blocks away, to instruct the older children. The children of the Zimmer Home attended school with non-orphaned children; the propaganda for the church states that "the entire environment is so arranged that the child experiences ordinary home life."

The home was primarily financed by the Bureau of Catholic Charities but also received donations from parents and outside benefactors. The nuns who worked there, however, received no salary—and were, in effect, indentured servants brought over from poor countries to work for nothing but room and board, caring for orphaned children.

"In the summer of 1961," states the church propaganda, "Rt. Rev. Msgr. Thomas M. Cullen initiated payment to the Sisters for their services at the Home. The first check for four of the six sisters arrived on January 1962." Prior to this arrangement, one imagines the women—poor immigrants—working virtually for free in the service of "poor, underprivileged Negro children."

In the brochure that I received about the home, the language is cloying and condescending—continually extolling the church for its service to these children.

One passage stands out to me though.

"For the first time in the history of Zimmer Home, the children were taken in February of 1963 to the fair grounds of the Pure Heart of Mary School, during Mardi Gras season to enjoy free amusement rides. They were transported by St. Peter Claver School Bus, generously donated by the Pastor of that parish. The merit for this treat belongs to the Knights of Peter Clavier.

"In concluding the Mardi Gras celebration, the children were permitted to occupy a roped in area in front of the Knights of Columbus Building, together with the white underprivileged children, to watch the festivities. However, when during the intermission the white children were taken to the American Legion Building for lunch, the group from Mobile was not permitted to enter because of the race distinction. Refreshments had to be brought to the children outside."

For the rest of my day, while driving around the city shopping for groceries, having coffee with a friend, I could not put this out of my mind—the image of the children of Zimmer waiting on the lawn to be served their lunch outside.

I knew I needed to make a trip down south, where my father had been born and raised, if I was to fill in many facts to his story. The problem was, I couldn't decide whether I should go alone or bring him along as a guide. He had already said he was willing. And I knew he could be a help in finding my way around—and in tracking down the people who had known him and his family while he was growing up. Without him, it was difficult to know where to begin. On the other hand, I had not spent time alone with my father very often in my life. Our fights over the years had been painful. I, out of the three children, had taken on my mother's rage as my own. I could not forgive and forget the ways he had hurt my mother or failed us as children when he was in the throes of his addiction, the ways he had failed to be a father, and I had a hard, prickly edge when talking to him. He was endlessly offering me bait for my blowups. And he was right: nothing he could do in the present would make up for his past sins, so he was in a hopeless situation when it came to me.

Our relationship seemed to function best through the conduit of e-mail, where he was reduced to a disembodied voice, or even less than that, a mind, sending interesting thoughts about impersonal subjects—politics, always politics—through the stratosphere.

I bought myself a ticket to New Orleans but spent the next few weeks hemming and hawing about whether to invite him to come with me. In fact, I waffled for so long that by the time I decided to buy him a ticket, it was less than a week before the scheduled trip. The ticket ended up costing three times the amount it should have.

It also required that my father take four different flights. He lives way up north in Saint John, New Brunswick, and the only ticket I could afford at that point required that he fly twice within Canada, and twice within the United States, before he finally arrived at the destination, the Louis Armstrong International Airport in New Orleans.

It was a zigzag of flights that moved him sideways, then diagonally, then back in the other direction again before he would finally land in New Orleans. He was quite good-natured about the fact and said he didn't care how many planes he had to get on as long as I was paying for everything—his travel, his meals, his hotel. So I went ahead and purchased the ticket.

Word spread quickly around my immediate family that I was going down south with him. My brother, Maceo, was bemused. He got along with my father better than I did and was the only one of us three kids who had traveled south with him to meet his family many years earlier.

My mother was surprised that I would dare to spend such intense time alone with him.

My sister was surprised too. A few days before the scheduled trip, my father forwarded me an e-mail he'd received from her with his own note to me attached: "What the hell is she talking about?"

Her e-mail to him was short and blunt. It was a chilling warning to my father not to go down south with me. She reminded him of an incident many years ago when she claimed I had tried to kill him with a butcher knife in Rhode Island where he was living at the time. She implied, in her e-mail, that I might try to do something like that again.

I knew the night she was referring to, over a decade earlier at his Rhode Island bachelor pad, but it wasn't true. I never tried to kill my father. She had the story wrong. It wasn't a butcher knife, it was a steak knife, something so blunt and small and serrated that it would have done little harm if I'd actually tried to stick it into him. The point is, I didn't do it. He came out of his bedroom, where he'd been locked for hours with a six-pack of beer, and stumbled toward the two of us, laughing. All around us were the abandoned chew toys of Mr. Briscoe, the mutt my father had found and neglected to care for and who had finally disappeared one day from his basement—either the dog had discovered a way out, or someone, a neighbor, a member of PETA, had taken pity and kidnapped the creature. In any case, my father held a beer can in one hand, the telephone in the other. My sister and I were stranded there at his house, and he was too drunk to drive us home to Boston or to a bus depot. We needed to call my mother for help, and he thought it was funny, a game, holding the phone receiver just out of my reach. I'd been there before, at the other end of his inebriation, but this time something inside me snapped. I held the knife gently to his chest and told him to give us the phone or else. His smile sort of faltered, and he handed me the phone and slurred something incomprehensible before stumbling back toward his bedroom.

He'd been so drunk then that now, sober, he didn't remember the night my sister was referring to, and I guess he decided she was kidding. I didn't correct him, and he agreed, rather cheerily, to go on the trip with me.

My father arrived in New Orleans the night before I did. I was to meet him at the boardinghouse where we were staying.

At the car rental agency, I was overtaken by a strange impulse, and despite my earlier concerns about money and budget, I asked to be upgraded from the modest midsize sedan I'd reserved to the biggest sport utility vehicle they had on the lot. I hadn't seen my father in years, and in my memory he was huge, too big to fit in an ordinary car. I drove the gleaming tank across the still dry and leveed city of New Orleans toward my father, where he waited in the French Quarter.

The last time I'd seen him I was living in Cambridge. He had showed up a day later than he said he would after driving all night. He arrived in a vehicle I'd never seen before, a pickup truck painted a nonfactory shade of turquoise. Irritated, I watched him from my window as he slid out the truck. I remember he appeared to bang his head on the door frame, but I didn't see him wince, so I wasn't sure if he'd hurt himself. Expressionless, he started across the street toward me, his head cocked to the side. He was dressed vaguely like a cowboy in boots, a floppy khaki jungle explorer hat and a black T-shirt with a tribal image emblazoned on it. He came through the door announcing he had business to take care of, would I mind if he used my phone? He then planted himself on my couch and began making calls, one after another. He seemed to grow larger the longer he sat there, and my apartment seemed to grow smaller around him. He stayed there all morning, a giant in a doll's house, his legs splayed out before him, talking to an old friend about a deal he had cooking with a television actor from the seventies he claimed to know.

He blew out of town the next day, leaving my bathroom littered with drugstore paraphernalia he'd forgotten to pack: an asthma inhaler, blood pressure medicine, and a tube of scar cream.

When I pulled up to the rambling white house, my father stood on the porch. He didn't look so large. In fact, he looked well. I was happy to see him. Inside, I found the place scattered with empty soda cans—he had already raided the minibar. The television was blaring the local news, sheets were rumpled on one of the beds, his luggage lay open, and his clothes were draped around. It was a mess. But he'd been busy. He'd wasted no time. He'd already called friends whom he hadn't spoken to in thirty years—people who could help us, help me understand the world in which he'd been raised. He had big plans for us, big plans. But he was hungry, he said, and he didn't have a dime. Could I take him out to lunch?

My father looks younger than his years. His face is almost entirely unlined. It's almost miraculous, given his years of heavy drinking and bad diet. When we are together, strangers often assume my father and I are a couple rather than father and daughter.

When I was in my early twenties, I was in the hospital for a few days following emergency ovarian surgery. I drifted in and out of delirium. When I woke on the second day, the Caribbean nurse told me that my "handsome boyfriend" had just been in for a visit. She said he'd just gone down to the cafeteria for some lunch and would be back soon. I didn't have a boyfriend at the time but was so confused by the drugs that I imagined I did, that I'd simply forgotten. Another nurse came in while I lay there waiting and said she'd also met my "handsome boyfriend." Whoever had been there had been flirting with the nurses. They were charmed. I lay there waiting to find out who my boyfriend was, trying to imagine who it might be, until my father walked in carrying a cup of coffee and a greasy muffin.

On our first day in New Orleans together, we went to a restaurant promising authentic New Orleans cooking. A table full of white men—dressed in dust-covered clothing, possibly construction workers on lunch break—looked up at us. Though they didn't say anything, they didn't really stop glaring at us until they finished their lunch and got up to leave the place. Their looks were decidedly hostile—overtly disgusted, as if they were fighting not to spit at us—and it struck me that to the outside world, we appeared to be not simply a couple but an interracial couple.

When the men were gone, my father said, "Did you pick up on that?"

I nodded. He was the one who had taught me to see these things with brutal clarity.

My father made a sound in his throat, but we didn't speak of it further.

———

On our second day in Louisiana, we drove out of New Orleans toward the bayou and the towns where my father had lived, on and off, as a young boy. We listened to zydeco music on that drive out of the city. I'd never heard it before. It was a thorny mix of Cajun, blues, and soul music. It was like the state of Louisiana itself, a bastard concoction, not quite American, not quite not. As the syncopated sounds of the accordion and the washboard played from the radio, a gravelly-voiced old man kept repeating the same pidgin phrase, lulling me into a kind of peaceful trance.

The music reminded me of how far I was from the place I'd been born, the stiffly stratified world of New England. I also felt how far I was from New York, the home I'd chosen after college. Out the window I took in the sights of the South: A Piggly Wiggly, a GOD IS WATCHING billboard, a Hardee's fast-food restaurant. An Indian bingo parlor behind a gas station.

Inside the car I felt a newfound affection blossoming for my father, a closeness to him that had eluded me my whole life. It was as if, down here, in the South, we were finally in a new space together. We were far from restraining orders and child support failures and the war-torn years of Boston. My father and I were friends, finally, bobbing our heads to the swamp music and headed on an adventure.

The music turned to static. My father switched around on the dial until he found a soul station. Barry White's "Can't Get Enough of Your Love" was playing: Barry White, that Walrus of Love, who had died the year before. Cause of death was a stroke due to high blood pressure. My father went quiet as we listened to the soul music. It is a song embedded in my earliest consciousness—a song my father used to play over and over again when I was little. It is a song that, listening to it now, seems strange in its inability to ever rise above the lead-in rambling, to ever become a song. Each time Barry White seems to move past his opening sweet nothings, every time he seems about to launch into actual singing, the meat of the song, the music peters out, and once again he's talking.

Barry White, along with Stevie Wonder and the Stylistics, made up the soundtrack to my early youth. Stevie and the Stylistics I associate with happy times, the grainy pastel colors of a washed-out seventies photograph. *Songs in the Key of Life. Betcha By Golly Wow.* Barry White, on the other hand, I associate with my most unhappy childhood memories. Barry White was one of the voices my father used to get drunk listening to in our living room on Robeson Street.

As we listened to him now, an air of thick melancholy fell over me, and when I looked at my father, he was frowning out at the road ahead. There were, I saw, tears in his eyes. I wondered if he was remembering what I was remembering. A few minutes before, listening to the zydeco music, that ugly past of ours seemed so far away, a traumatic era that had been safely put to rest. But now, in the deep voice of Barry White, it had swum back to us.

"What are you thinking?" I asked my father. And I thought maybe this was the time for it—for us to finally talk in a spirit of truth and reconciliation, in a spirit of remorse and forgiveness, about the past.

My father looked at me. "He died too young. Shit. Why'd he have to go like that?"

It took me a moment to understand—to register that he was upset not about our family's past but about Barry White. He was crying about the death of the singer. And my father began to speak, giving a long slow eulogy for the man; he referred to him as "Barry," as if they were old friends. He said Barry, born the same year he was, had come from the same part of the country as he had—had sprung out of the same poverty-stricken, segregated black society that he had sprung out of. My father's voice cracked with emotion as he spoke about the success of a black man who had come from nothing to make music that had traveled the world. My father said that when he had traveled to Egypt a few years before, he had seen Barry White's music being sold on the streets of Cairo.

"On the streets of Cairo," my father reiterated, staring out at the freeway ahead.

This to my father was the definitive sign of success—that Barry White, a man from his same background, from the Deep South, from his generation, had gotten all the way to Egypt.

Some of the best and the brightest black men of my father's generation left the country and never came back. For a long time, the bulk of my childhood, both my father's siblings lived outside the country—in Canada and in France. Only my father remained in America, in Boston no less. Only my father married the most American of spouses, a daughter of the American Revolution. Now, divorced, in debt, perhaps twenty years after he should have, he too has finally fled the country. He lives in Canada, married to a Canadian. He spends his time trying to figure out ways to get even farther away from the United States, to the Middle East, to Egypt, yes, and neighboring countries where he has made an odd assortment of friends. My father is never as happy, never as lighthearted, as he is after one of his jaunts to the Middle East. There he is free. There he blends into the crowds of Arab faces. There in the outside world he is no longer limited by the racialized thinking that wraps itself like barbed wire around his mind.

In college my boyfriend was the son of a Jewish man and a black woman. His father was a third-world economist, and my boyfriend spent his childhood in New York City, Kenya, Bangladesh, and Puerto Rico. This boyfriend fascinated me in that we were both biracial and yet had such completely opposite experiences. He had none of my bitterness, none of my anger about whiteness and racism, none of my sense of conflict between my two sides. He was something I'd never met, a mixed-race person proud of both his heritages, whose parents were still married and still in love. I remember the first time I saw his parents. They walked in the door of our dormitory, an elegant honey-colored black woman wearing a short Afro and flowing foreign fabrics, and a handsome blue-eyed, silver-haired father. They moved through the lobby as one entity and greeted their dreadlocked son. I had never seen anything like it, and for a moment jealousy moved through me like a hot flash. Something I had thought was impossible was indeed possible. I asked myself later, over lunch with them, whether it was a function of these parents' genders that made their relationship work so much better than my parents'; was it that the black person in the union was the woman and the white person was the man, and not vice versa, that made it work? Or perhaps it was that the white person was not a Wasp but a Jew? I had adopted my father's way of thinking—to read everyone as a representative of a group, as proof of their group characteristics, rather than seeing this couple as two individuals who had somehow, through luck and through will, pulled off a successful marriage, no mean feat for anybody in their generation, regardless of race. Instead I wanted to be able to categorize them, to analyze them using the tools of race and sociology.

It was not just my father's way of thinking. It was my

mother's too. Years later, the summer after my college graduation, I moved to New York with this boyfriend, and we lived on the first floor of his family home. I studied his parents during that summer, still awed by the existence of a happy, unified interracial family. They glittered to me, like something otherworldly. One night my mother and my brother drove down from Boston to see me and meet the other family. They arrived at the house after dark, and I remember opening the door and seeing them standing there on the doorstep, my single white mother standing beside my lanky, light-skinned, half-nappy-haired brother, realizing only at the sight of them how much I had missed them and just how alienated I had felt in the happiness of this surrogate family. My mother wore a shabby wool coat and carried a bag of McDonald's garbage, and she walked in cursing about traffic. My brother looked sheepish and cynical as he sat in the living room, surrounded by this family's artifacts from around the world.

After their visit my mother and I met for lunch the next day in Greenwich Village, and she seemed to feel the need to defend herself.

"The only interracial couples from my generation who survived left the country," she said. "That's what his parents did right. They left the country."

Years later I tried to leave the country. I lived in London, where my friends were black people from around the world. I remember noticing that they lacked the black American bitterness—and more importantly, that quintessentially American obsession with race. They told me they didn't understand why we—black Americans—were so hung up on it, why we saw it everywhere, in everything. They were right: like those religious fanatics who see Jesus' face in clouds and window fog and rock formations, we did see it everywhere. I remember feeling so lonely in the presence of these seemingly enlightened, unfettered foreign black people, and realizing that at the end of the day I felt at home only in the prison of America. Only there did I make sense.

Our first stop was Houma, a bayou town where my father had spent a period of months as a boy. He wanted to show me the house where he'd lived, the school he'd attended. But it was lunchtime when we got there and we were both famished, so first we went searching for soul food. We wanted the real deal: cornbread and grits and blackened catfish and fried chicken and jambalaya. My father slowed the car every time we saw a black person and asked them where we could get some lunch. The only two white people we'd stopped to ask about lunch had suggested Subway. All the black people had the same answer: Bubba's was the place. Bubba's was what we were looking for. But they each gave us a different set of directions for how to get there, and every time we tried to find the place, we ended up nowhere, in a cul-de-sac, or on the edge of town where the shops ended and the freeway began.

My father, as we drove around Houma looking for Bubba's, spoke about the black society of his youth. He said the idea of family he grew up with was more fluid than it was in the white world. Black Americans—in the midst of Jim Crow, on the heels of slavery, where family units were decimated by that so-called benevolent patriarchy—had to invent a more creative definition of family. Segregation, the American racial caste system, set black people up to consider one another "brothers and sisters" whether or not theirs was a truly biological relation. In his childhood, my father had followed his mother in her peripatetic journey from the Louisiana bayou to Montgomery, Alabama, to New York City, and ultimately to Boston—sometimes living with her as a family, more often than not being shunted off onto strangers.

The woman my father named me after is not related to him by blood. Emma Danzy and her husband, Saxton Danzy, were two in the cast of characters who took my father into their homes during an essentially homeless childhood. My sister is named after yet another one of these adoptive relatives, a woman named Ann-Lucien Green, a fat woman with a short temper who came to fetch my father and his siblings from the orphanage.

In Houma, my father said, they had lived with a woman he can remember only as being called "Ma Verrett." He remembered her as a kind, elderly woman, a fading beauty with Indian blood who would brush and brush her long, straight, once-black silver hair before going to bed each night. She was, it was rumored, the mistress to a rich white senator. He and his siblings stayed with her for a period he remembers fondly. They felt more at home in Louisiana—where their light skin and mixed features were common—than they did in more rigid and starkly segregated Alabama. We forgot about our hunger, forgot about Bubba's for a moment, as my father talked and drove, squinting out at the streets, trying to locate something familiar, the place he'd lived briefly as a child with the old woman with the long silver hair.

And then, somehow, we were there. We were on the street. He recognized it because of the graveyard where he used to play.

It was still there. And next to the graveyard was a field of dried-out grass. It sat at the edge of a hospital and a parking structure. Ma Verrett's house where he had spent that period of his child-hood used to sit in this field. It was gone, razed. There was a small shack there, a neighbor's home he remembered, still stand-ing. It looked odd beside the giant hospital wing. We wandered around the nearby graveyard looking for the gravestone of Ma Verrett. We split up. I took the left side of the graveyard, and my father took the right side. When I was halfway through my side, my father approached me to say that he'd just remembered something: this was a white graveyard. No black bodies were buried in this plot of ground. In death, the bodies were divided as in life. Which meant Ma Verrett, the half-Indian, half-black concubine of a rich white senator, had to be buried somewhere else. We wouldn't find her here, no matter how long we looked.

We could not find Bubba's, and the lunch hour was melting into late afternoon. We were getting weak as our blood sugar levels dropped. Our earlier irritation had given way to a dazed bewilderment as we drove those Houma streets one last time, scanning the storefronts for the magic and elusive soul of soul food.

I had argued for Subway an hour earlier, but my father was stubborn. He wanted authentic or nothing. He pulled our car up beside a woman on the sidewalk, a middle-aged black woman, weary-eyed, with a little boy at her side.

"We're looking for soul food," he said. "Where can we get some soul food?"

"Oh, you're lookin' for Bubba's," the woman said.

He said yes, that was what we wanted, Bubba's. And I listened as she gave my father yet another set of directions to what was beginning to seem like a practical joke. In my delirium, I remembered a short story that every American high school student reads, Shirley Jackson's "The Lottery," and I imagined us finally finding the restaurant filled with all the people we'd asked for directions, only to be pelted to our death with old stale pieces of biscuit.

It sounded so simple. Two blocks ahead, take a right, the woman was saying, then your first left, go under the freeway, hang a roscoe, and you'll see it. A shack. With the best soul food Louisiana has to offer.

We set off once again and once again found ourselves lost, still hungry, going in circles.

As we headed back to town, I saw up ahead, on the side of the road, a cabin with a sign over the door that read: ABEAR'S CAFÉ—CAJUN MEALS, ALLIGATOR, RED BEANS, RICE. It was a roadside diner with a cluster of semis and pickup trucks parked out front. I pointed toward it. My father had explained to me earlier, lectured me really, on the difference between Cajuns and Creoles. One was white and one was black, but I couldn't remember what else separated them or if their food was different. "What about that place?" I said, my mouth watering. He slowed, squinted, and then turned into the driveway. "I guess we can give it a try."

We walked through the door and into a sea of whiteness. Every face in the joint turned to look at us. I saw what they saw: a young white woman with her older black boyfriend. It was unsettling to imagine that we looked that way, but to strangers I knew we did. My father looked young for his age, and perhaps I looked old for my age, I wasn't sure. And the fact was, nobody thought we looked related. So what else would they assume? I hesitated at the doorway beside my father, imagining silence falling over the joint, that trucker there standing up and saying, *You're dead meat, nigger*. I imagined the familiar scene from so many movies about the South, the white-hooded Klan members chasing us through the forest, hounds nipping at my heels. But after a beat people returned to their food, and the room was filled with the pleasant hum of conversation. An elderly woman led us to a table and gave us our menus, and we studied them. My father claimed he was going to practice restraint and order a bowl of gumbo, but when the waitress came back he ordered the combination platter, the fattiest dish on the menu, instead. I followed at a close second with the fried catfish with a side of fries. We cleaned our plates in silence.

Afterward, in the car, my father said, "Food wasn't bad." Then he turned on the radio and found the music. We were quiet as we drove on the main road back into town, toward the freeway entrance. We were headed to Jennings, the town where my father was born. We were late, there were people expecting us there, a family of high yellow Creoles Anna had lived with when my father was born, but whose relationship to her he was, once again, not clear on. They'd been expecting us over an hour ago, so we should have been in a hurry, but my father drove slowly through the center of town. When I turned to look at him, I saw he was scanning the street signs, still searching for Bubba's, though we'd already eaten.

Jennings, Louisiana. What was the significance of our next stop? From the bits and pieces my father knew, Anna, pregnant with him, had come back to the South from New York City, bereft and traumatized after whatever happened with the elusive Mexican boxer, Francisco José. She came to Louisiana and lived there with a group of Creoles whose relationship to her was never clear to my father.

Growing up, my father had told me about this big family of Creoles, and the bayou where he'd lived on and off throughout his childhood. He talked about it with reverence and affection. Louisiana was the source of happy memories for my father. It was the source of the only part of his identity for which he seemed to have unfettered affection—and that he celebrated every time he made us gumbo or jambalaya.

Earlier in the day, from our room in the inn, my father had called information and tracked down the members of the family who had taken Anna in for his birth. To my amazement, they still lived in Jennings and were happy to hear from my father after all these years. They were expecting us that afternoon, apparently with open arms. But we meandered so much on our way, looking for Bubba's, that by the time we got there, the light was already dimming, a February silver glow of the sun as we drove alongside the bayou and followed signs to Jennings.

It was in my mind much larger than what it turned out to be. We crossed a train track and passed a wood mill and came to a desolate cluster of houses surrounded by woods. There were no businesses or large houses. Just dilapidated shacks and one-level ranch houses.

My father squinted, trying to find the house he'd known in his youth. He pointed to a small, modest white clapboard cottage. "There it is," he said, and we pulled into the driveway. He leaped out of the car and began snapping photographs. After a few minutes an elderly white woman came out of the house and asked him what he was doing. I sat in the car watching, nervous, while he spoke to the woman on her lawn. She relaxed and pointed off down the road. He returned to the car and told me it was the wrong house. Now he wasn't sure which one it was. In any case, she'd pointed him in the direction of the family he'd known, the Creoles who were expecting us. And so we drove down the block to a tiny shack on the corner. A man came outside and approached us in the driveway as we were getting out, a man about my father's age, with light skin and a sweet, rather sad face. He and my father embraced, and my father introduced him to me.

We followed the man inside. They were all waiting for us, excited, and I realized my father was a celebrity to them, an important success story—somebody who had made it out. They had heard word over the years of his publications and his adventures. They had heard of me too, had seen mention of my books in various magazines, and were delighted when I handed them a copy of my first novel, and asked me to sign it. They were a whole clan of Louisiana Creoles, on the fault line of the races. They showed me a photograph of the family from earlier, happier times, a giant clan of high yellow daughters and the one handsome son standing on a lawn, smiling, young and hopeful and strong.

Now they sat crowded into this tiny, cluttered space, a place they had known their whole life but had perhaps never expected to stay in—two sisters and an old woman who was the last survivor of her generation of sisters.

She had been a contemporary of Anna. She told us of the great sadness of her life: a few years earlier she had answered the door to learn that her grandson had killed himself. She kept bringing it up, the death of this grandson. She told me Anna was a lovely woman, so intelligent. I asked her what the connection was between Anna and her family, and she just smiled and said, Father Ryan.

The deep Catholicism of my father's youth was becoming increasingly clear to me—the link, like this name, Father Ryan, between all the disparate parts.

We sat for a long time and talked while my father snapped photographs, and I found myself growing older and sadder as I looked at the kind faces of these people and thought about how my father had made it out of the South, how his gifted and accomplished mother had made it along with her half-orphaned, half-caste children out of the provinciality of this world, made it to something not exactly better, the hard northern housing projects.

On my last day with my father in New Orleans, I drove him to the airport where he would return to Canada, to his life in the suburban outpost of Saint John, New Brunswick, to a context far removed from the world he had known as a boy in the South.

I was getting tired of paying for him. For four days I'd been covering his airfare, food, lodging, and everything in between, including souvenirs to take home with him. But I was focusing on the positive: We had survived the four days without any major conflicts. We had not always gotten along, but we had shared something, and I felt closer to him.

At the airport loading zone where we idled, he turned to me. I thought he was going to thank me for the trip or say something about what we'd shared.

Instead, he asked if I could spare forty dollars. He said he had not one dollar on him and didn't want to travel empty-handed.

Money—his need for it, his attitude that he was somehow entitled to mine—had been an issue between us before. The first time it came up was many years earlier when I found a publisher for my first novel. Excited, proud, I told my father—and mentioned the amount of money I'd gotten from the publisher for the book. It was my life's dream to be a writer, and I wanted him to be happy for me. Instead, he spent days calling me with increasing desperation and hostility, demanding that I loan him money. He claimed it was an emergency, and when I said no, he accused me of being tightfisted, cold, like my Wasp family. When I finally buckled under and loaned him the money, it was thousands of dollars—but a few thousand less than what he'd asked for. He barely thanked me and seemed affronted that I'd not given him the full amount. He'd promised he would pay me back in weeks but didn't actually return the money for many years.

I swallowed, hoping my silence would give him the message that I'd had enough. There is nothing quite like the feeling of shelling out money to the man who skipped out on your child support and contributed nothing to your college tuition. But the minutes ticked past, and I realized he wasn't going to get out of the car until I gave him the money. I finally gave him two twenties, swearing to myself that this would never happen again.

We didn't say goodbye. I said, "Just go."

When he leaned in to kiss my cheek, I moved out of reach.

Afterward I sat in the SUV watching him walk off with my forty dollars and his bags toward the fluorescent lights of the airport, tears of something—rage, sadness, love, disgust, pity, exhaustion—streaming down my face. I whispered, through those tears, over and over again, "I'm sorry." It was a sorry to my sister, my brother, and me—not us now, but to us then, when we were children. And it was an apology, as well, to my father, not to him now but to him then, as a child. I watched him walk away, through the sliding doors and into the fluorescent light of the airport. I expected him to turn and give me one last look, but he didn't. I started the engine and drove away.

I was on my own, for better or for worse. I sped in my SUV north on the I-10 toward Montgomery, Alabama. The relatives I had never known growing up were expecting me for dinner.

I was on schedule, making good time, but there was one bit of business I had to take care of on the way. I had to make a detour I had promised my father I would make.

That morning, before we set off for the airport, he had scribbled down the names of two women he'd known fifty-four years earlier, Ernestine and Clementine Hurston, twin sisters who had lived in the Zimmer Home while he and his siblings were there. He told me to look them up. He gave me the name of the church that the orphanage had been affiliated with and told me that the church might help me find the two women he'd known so long ago. It was a crazy tip, preposterously far-fetched, but my father insisted I follow it, and I promised him I would.

I passed through Mississippi and into Alabama, and after a while I saw signs for Prichard, the town my father had scribbled on the paper, where the Zimmer Home had been—the place that had been, according to my father and J, the site of unspeakable acts of cruelty and impropriety toward children.

In Prichard I found myself in the center of what looked like the end of the world. It was a Sunday, and I thought at first that was why all the shops looked closed. But as I cruised down Main Street, I saw that in fact most of the storefronts were boarded up. I drove slowly, looking for a sign of human life, but found only a wide and desolate main street with a long road of empty businesses. I had never been to a town that seemed quite so economically and culturally depressed. Later, I did research on Prichard, Alabama, and learned it had been the location of a powerful event in American history. It is hard to believe, looking at it now, but it was once known as "Africatown," and had been founded by a group of Ghanaians who were brought to this country as slaves in 1859. Slave trading had been outlawed at that point for almost fifty years, but rogue traders brought the slaves in a secret voyage. The federal authorities were waiting to arrest them when they arrived in Mobile Harbor one night, but they docked offshore and put the slaves on a riverboat and sent them into hiding before burning and sinking their own schooner. After the Civil War, the original group of intended slaves created their own village in Prichard. There they continued to speak their own language, had disputes arbitrated by their tribal chieftain, and had their illnesses treated by a traditional African doctor. Up until World War II, Africatown existed as a self-contained community.

But as I drove those desolate streets in search of life, I saw no visible signs of this history anywhere. I called information on my cell phone asking for the phone number of Ernestine Hurston, but the operator had no listing for such a person. Relieved, having fulfilled my promise, I was about to give up and get back on the freeway when, up ahead, I saw a parking lot filled with cars and people, young men and women who stood in clusters smoking and talking. I thought as I drove toward it that it must be a restaurant serving Sunday brunch, or maybe it was the parking lot to a church. But as I got closer, I saw the sign over a building in the lot: it was a tax and loan center—packed. This was where the town's action was. I parked and went inside and found a room filled with rows of people sitting waiting for their number to be called so they could speak to a loan representative. They looked up at me from their chairs in the waiting area with curiosity. I could see that I looked like a foreigner to them. It wasn't my physical appearance, or racial features, but something far more profound that separated me from the people in that room. I had traveled far and wide, and these people had not. They had never left the place they were born into. This was the world my father grew up inside. Until his mother became a traveler. Until his mother broke from the nest and moved away from her roots, as frayed and fragile as they were. It was she who in some sense began the family tradition of marrying outside one's own kind, of leaving home, of becoming rootless, a wanderer.

I told a young woman—a loan officer, I suppose—at one of the desks that I was looking for a church. I told her the name of it. She frowned and said it sounded familiar. Then she asked the people at the desks around her. Did anybody know of a Catholic church around here?

A lone woman in one of the folding chairs raised her hand and said her cousin Shirley attended that church.

It sat at the end of a street with squalid, crumbling homes. It looked like a million other Catholic churches—gray brick, a towering fortress, depressing. As I pulled into the parking lot, I had little hope that it would offer any leads. Here was a church that had once been affiliated with an orphanage, but that was half a century ago, and it didn't necessarily bring me any closer to finding the twin sisters who had known my father once upon a time.

It was Sunday and church was in session, judging from the cars that crowded the parking lot. It was almost noon. I sat in the parking lot just staring at the exterior of the church's stained-glass windows. The exhaustion of my past few days with my father was catching up with me. I had plenty of friends who had written off their fathers for far lesser crimes than mine had committed. They didn't necessarily disown their fathers, though some did. They just didn't make an effort to know them anymore.

And when I thought about it, it was so thin, the remaining connection between this man and me. The little girl who had lived at his mercy was gone. I had survived him. I had endured him.

So why was I here, hundreds of miles from the comforts of my home, in a parking lot to a Catholic church in dirt-poor Prichard, Alabama, formerly known as Africatown, searching for a witness who had known my father fifty-plus years ago?

Why did I need to understand the reasons for his behavior? The fact of his behavior was enough. After the age of thirty nobody gets the excuse of a bad childhood anymore. The statute of limitations has passed.

A door opened, and I watched the parishioners flood out into the parking lot. They were joking and laughing, mostly black but with enough white people to call it a mixed crowd, all ages. True multiculturalism, my father once pointed out to me, flourishes in only four places: drug dens, casinos, the military—and last but not least, houses of God (mosques, churches, Jim Jones's Guyanese retreat).

I watched them emerge and stand around chatting in the parking lot, saw some of them throw me curious looks where I sat idling in the SUV. My presence here was so random as to be ridiculous. I had to remind myself why I'd just gotten off the freeway to come to this strange town. The Hurston girls—the wild-goose chase my father had sent me on. Of course, they wouldn't still be living here, in the town where they'd been orphaned fifty-four years earlier. But I was here. I could say I'd made the effort. I opened the car door and stepped out into the muted late-February light.

Something happens to me in churches. Something has always happened to me in churches. It's either a psychosomatic response to religion, or an allergic reaction to incense. Whatever the case, I begin to yawn. It sounds harmless enough, but it's on the level of a seizure—a kind of ceaseless gasping for air that doesn't stop until I've stepped out of the doors of the church. My body begs for oxygen and doesn't stop until I'm down the steps.

As I stepped inside the church in Prichard, Alabama, I felt it starting up. The hallway was empty except for an elderly man carrying a box of votive candles out of the worship area. He saw me standing there yawning in the hallway and asked if I needed help.

"Is there a priest I can talk to?"

"Sure honey, the priest is in a meeting right now. Just inside those doors." He pointed to a set of glass doors a bit farther down the hall, and I saw a seminar room where a motley group of people sat around a table. At the front of the table was an old white man in a priest's black suit.

I took a seat outside the door. I heard muted laughter. I squirmed, yawned so hard tears streamed down my face as I waited for the priest to emerge from his meeting. After a while he did, tottering, sunken faced, ancient, and Irish.

I told him I was looking for two people who had many decades ago lived in the Zimmer Home. I waited for his reaction of confusion at worst, amusement at best. Instead he just nodded and said, "Yes, the Zimmer Home."

I continued. "I'm looking for two women who lived there over fifty years ago. Ernestine and Clementine Hurston?"

To my surprise, he nodded. "Sure. Clementine goes to church these days in the next town over. She moved, you know. But Ernestine was at mass this morning. Come up the hill with me, and I'll give you her phone number."

Stunned, I followed him across the street and up a small slope to a brick building, his living quarters.

There in the dusty front room he fumbled through some files and found the numbers. With trembling fingers, he wrote out the new names of both sisters—they had both married— and their phone numbers on a white index card.

I called Ernestine from the parking lot of the church.

A woman answered on the third ring, sounding harried, tired.

"Hello," I asked. "Is this Ernestine?"

"Yes."

I swallowed, suddenly nervous. It was of course amazing that I'd found her so easily, and that she was still attending the same church that ran the orphanage where she'd lived fifty years before. But I didn't know why she would remember my father, who had lived in the orphanage a few years and then left, and whom she hadn't heard from in half a century.

"My father asked me to contact you. His name is Carl Senna? He knew you a long—"

Before I could continue, she cut me off. "Carl Senna?"

"Yes, from the Zimmer Home."

She moaned. "My God. Good lord. I've been looking for your daddy for the past fifty years. I don't believe this. Carl is your father? Where are you calling from?"

I told her I was sitting in the parking lot of the church she'd attended that morning. She laughed, sobbed a little, told me I had to come to her house *now*. She didn't even ask why I was calling. She didn't seem confused. Only thrilled that I had tracked her down.

She said I'd never find her house on my own. The directions were too complicated, so we agreed to meet at a McDonald's off a nearby freeway exit. She arrived a few minutes after me—a plump, pleasant-looking woman with smooth brown skin, a vibrant smile. She wore a denim jacket, jeans, and sneakers. I went out into the sunlight to meet her, and she opened her arms and embraced me as if she'd been waiting for me, not just my father, to come see her all these years. She spoke in a rush about how miraculous it was that I had found her. She said that after she'd gotten off the phone with me, she had called her twin sister, Clementine, to tell her that Carl's daughter had called her out of the blue, *Carl's* daughter, and they were both reeling over the miracle of God's ways. Because they'd never stopped wondering all these years, Whatever happened to those Senna children?

I followed her sedan through a series of winding roads that led deeper and deeper into the back woods of Alabama until we reached her house—a trailer on bricks in the center of a clearing of trees.

She explained that her real house had been destroyed in a fire many months earlier and that she was using the insurance money to build a new home. She seemed quite cheerful about the fire; she spoke about it as if it had come as an opportunity to rebuild rather than a tragedy. The construction was ongoing.

Inside, the trailer didn't feel temporary. It was neat and homey, with animal-print-patterned blankets thrown over leather furniture, and a giant painting of Malcolm X over the mantelpiece. On the sofa sat two adolescent girls sipping sodas.

Ernestine held my arm and introduced me to them. "This is Danzy. Her father and I lived in the Zimmer Home together. Remember I told you about the Zimmer Home?"

The girls nodded, intrigued. "Yeah, that's where you grew up."

"Well, Carl and his siblings were there with me. And his daughter, she came all the way from New York to meet me." Ernestine led me into the kitchen area. "Those are my neighbor's kids," she told me. "They come over just to hang out. Everybody feels like my home is their home, because it is."

I sat with Ernestine at the kitchen table. We sipped soda and talked about the past. She said she'd years ago been trying to put together a commemorative book—kind of like a yearbook—of all the kids who lived in the Zimmer Home, and that my father and his siblings were the only children she couldn't track down.

She told me that she and her sister, Clementine, were the two children who had lived in the Zimmer Home the longest. They were brought there as infants and stayed all the way through high school—the totality of their childhood. They watched the other children, like my father and his siblings, come and go, and they remained, the permanent fixtures inside those walls. They were twin sisters who didn't know who their birth parents were or why they'd been abandoned. But, she said, the Zimmer Home had become a home to them as much as any other home, and she thought of the children who lived there with them as siblings.

And indeed, unlike my father, she spoke of the Zimmer Home fondly. She brought out the makeshift yearbook she'd put together, and it was full of sentimental remembrances like any other school yearbook. My father and his siblings were the only ones missing from the photographs.

She said she remembered the Senna kids so well. She had never, in fact, forgotten them. She said they had arrived one day out of nowhere, three beautiful mixed-looking children. She said there were a lot of mixed kids in the home, because at that time mixed kids just *happened*, the evidence of secret lives that nobody wanted to acknowledge, and so the parents got rid of the kids. She said my father was a genius. He could read and write before anybody else and was always off somewhere in a corner, reading. And the baby girl, she was too cute for words. She said she remembered their mother would come and visit some weekends, and that the nuns would gather all the children to hear Mrs. Senna play the piano.

I listened, trying to hear hints of the "horror" that my father and the other former resident, J, had described.

I told her I had spoken to my father and J about their experiences. "They don't have good memories of the place."

Until then Ernestine had been smiling, rapturous, as she described the place that had raised her. But something stiffened in her features. "They said that?"

Her smile was still there, but it was stiff, plastic. It was as if her feelings were hurt by their recollection.

"They said the nuns didn't treat the kids well."

She sighed and shrugged. "Well, yeah, I mean, those nuns, they could whip you good."

"They said it wasn't just whipping."

"Oh yeah, they used to call us names. Sister Margaret and some of the others. The things that came out of their mouths." She giggled, but her eyes were growing more anxious, less friendly, darting around the room. "Some of them were real mean."

I told her about J. I told her he had spent a whole lifetime trying to recover from what had happened to him there.

She looked down at the handmade yearbook in her hands. "Well, I don't know, because they never brought me upstairs. See, I was real wild. Always talking back." She said J was different. "He was so sweet, so they used to take him upstairs with them. It was 'cause he was so sweet."

"What do you mean?" I asked. "What was upstairs?"

She fingered the edge of the yearbook she'd put together as she spoke. "They would bring him up there to where they slept. But they didn't bring me up there. I was too wild. They didn't bring me upstairs."

"What do you mean?"

She looked at me suddenly, and her face—which had looked

75

to me so bright and cheerful moments before—was filled with sadness. "It was the only home me and Clementine ever knew. It was home for us. The Zimmer Home was our family. They took us in, and we never knew anywhere else."

Just then the door opened, and a young man came in wearing rubber work overalls.

Ernestine seemed relieved and leaped up to greet him.

"This is my son, Charlie. Charlie, you won't believe who this is. Come meet her. Charlie, this is Danzy. Her daddy is Carl. I've told you about him."

Charlie smiled, nodding. "From the Zimmer Home?"

My father, until the week before, had never spoken to me about the orphanage. And he'd certainly never mentioned Ernestine or her sister until this week, when I was about to go to Alabama. But to Ernestine, he'd existed as a persistent character in the stories she'd told her children of her youth in the Zimmer Home. Of course, he'd stayed only three years, until his relatives came to claim him—so the orphanage was not all he knew, or all he had. For Ernestine, it was all the identity she had as a child.

She was going on now to her son about me. "She's like family, Charlie. Her daddy sent her here because he wanted her to meet me." She looked at me. "I tell my children, anybody who lived in the Zimmer Home with me is family. That's right. Family. You're family. That means she's your family too, Charlie."

For the next fifteen minutes we took photographs together as if I really were a long-lost cousin, Charlie and me in front of the Malcolm X painting, Ernestine and me in front of the panther statue.

She kept talking about my father's genius, how he was a prodigy and all the nuns knew it. She talked about how pretty my father's little sister was and how she bet she'd grown up into a great beauty.

Outside by my car, Ernestine and Charlie and the neighborhood girls crowded around while I pulled out a photograph I had of Anna. Ernestine stared at it for a moment, in silence, and nodded, a shadow of sadness crossing her face once again. She said she remembered that face, she remembered that woman. "She was thin and dark, and she played the piano so beautifully, it made the nuns cry."

Before I got in the car, Ernestine told me what she said was one of the saddest memories from her childhood, the day my father and his siblings disappeared. One moment they were all playing outside on the lawn with her and the other kids, like normal, and the next moment a nun had come to fetch my father and his siblings and asked them to come inside to the office. Somebody was here to see them. Ernestine said she never saw them again. She said she and the other children cried that night when the nuns informed them that the Senna children were gone for good. She said she kept asking the nuns the rest of the week, "Aren't they ever coming back? Ever?"

I thought about that last detail as I drove through a clearing in the woods and onto the main road back to the freeway. I tried to imagine my father as a child, one moment standing on the patchy lawn with the other children of Zimmer, the next moment, gone.

My father, in one of our many recent conversations about his childhood, told me that he thought the biggest casualty of slavery was the black family. He said the violence against that institution created damage the effects of which have persisted long after slavery was eradicated. "But the saving grace was the way people turned to each other electively," my father told me over the phone one night. "They embraced each other despite the proof of blood linkage. We were denied what white families had, the dignity of knowing our antecedents, of knowing who our mother and father were, so it was love that brought us together in the end and made us hold on to one another."

Ernestine and I said goodbye with hugs and kisses. She said I was family now, Zimmer family, and to remember that. But as I drove off the property, away from the trailer park and the big burned square of land, I was sure I'd never see her again.

My father had a different version of the same story of what he called his "liberation" from the Zimmer Home. Ernestine's saddest memory turned out to be one of my father's happiest memories from his childhood. He said Anna had not been to visit them at the home for a long time. Then one day—that day they were out playing on the lawn with Ernestine and the other children—a nun came to fetch him. She told them there was a woman inside who claimed to be their family member and who was coming to take them home. The nuns asked the children to go into a room and tell her if they recognized the woman. The story suggests that Anna was not reachable even to verify to the nuns that the people coming to claim her children were relatives.

My father and his siblings promised they would tell the nuns if they didn't recognize the woman. They went into a room and there sat their aunt, Ann-Lucien—a big-boned gruff woman they'd loved and feared on Ripley Street in Montgomery in the years before the Zimmer Home. My father says that he and his siblings ran to her, and "we were all over her, hugging and kissing her," and that this was why years later he named his firstborn child—my sister—after the woman who had come to save them from the orphanage that day.

When I spoke to my father later and told him about the encounter with Ernestine, he seemed neither surprised nor impressed that I'd been able to track her down. He had suspected that she would still be living in the proximity of the church and the Zimmer Home. He had understood something I did not: that in the world of the rural South, in the world of the disenfranchised people he grew up with, the town you were born in and raised in was the same town you died in. He understood that he was different from the other children in the Zimmer Home, that he—who had written books and traveled around the world—was an improbable exception to the rule. I was only beginning to understand just how much of an anomaly my father was, how miraculous his trajectory was, from orphan of the Zimmer Home in Prichard, Alabama, to the life he came to live at the height of his success.

Ernestine had made this starkly clear to me in a way that nothing before her and nothing since her has.

I asked him where Anna had been living those years they were at the Zimmer Home; why she had to leave them there. He could only quote from the letter that the Catholic Charities sent him years later when he wrote asking for information. Later he sent me a copy of the letter.

Dear Mr. Senna:

I checked your family record as you requested. I must admit that there is minimal information.

According to the record, your mother came to Catholic Charities on August 25, 1949, requesting placement for her

three children. Her husband had abandoned her. Your
mother claimed that your father drank and never supported
his family adequately. Your mother had been teaching at St.
John's School in Montgomery, however, they did not need
her any longer. She was then offered a teaching position in
Houma, Louisiana, but needed to have a home for her
children before she could accept the position. Your mother
was most desirous of pursuing her college education. She
felt that an education would enable her to get a good job
and eventually be able to provide a home for her children.

Yet when my father and his siblings were finally retrieved from
the orphanage, it was not by Anna, who had at this point already received her degree from the school she'd apparently
left them there to attend, Xavier University in New Orleans.
She was nowhere to be found. His aunt, Ann-Lucien, came to
retrieve them instead. She brought them back to the house in
Montgomery where Anna had been raised. It was the only con-
sistent home any of them had known. Anna had left this home
and was off somewhere, nobody knew where. Now here were
her children, tarnished and bedraggled after three years in a
Catholic orphanage.

According to my aunt Betty Jean, when Ann-Lucien arrived
home with the three would-be orphans, the family was upset by
how the children had changed in their years away. They looked
unkempt, rough. Ann-Lucien immediately went out to buy
each of them a pair of new shoes.

I drove onto the freeway north to Montgomery, toward the
home to which Ann-Lucien had brought the children after rescuing them from the orphanage, still amazed that in the past

few hours I'd not only located Ernestine Hurston but had sat in her kitchen, discussing the distant past. Yet as I solved one mystery, another seemed to open up before me.

Anna came to visit her children, to play the piano in front of the white nuns and their "unfortunate negro" charges, yet she could not bring her children home with her. What made it so impossible for her to care for them? Was it her quest for an education—for a better life, a good teaching job—that kept her away? Or something else?

I arrived in Montgomery after dark and checked into the Embassy Suites, a mammoth and sparkling hotel in the center of town. It had come recommended to me by Betty Jean Foy. She was the last surviving member of her generation. In her eighties, she lived in the same house on South Ripley Street where she and Anna grew up. I had not known her in my childhood, but when I had spoken to her months earlier, from my apartment in Brooklyn, she kept calling me "baby." When I asked her if I could come visit her she said, "Anytime, baby, anytime."

I loved the way she said "baby," the way she said my name, a Creole name, a Southern black name. She had said it in a slow drawl, the way it was meant to be spoken.

I wasn't sure what my relationship was to Betty Jean.

My father and I, on our last night in Louisiana together, had had dinner at a famous Creole restaurant in New Orleans called Dooky Chase. There, over gumbo and catfish, my father had tried to explain his mother's relationship to Betty Jean and her people. They were family and they were not family. Anna was, he said, the daughter of a woman whose name was Goldie Gadson. This name was all he or Anna knew of her birth mother, he said, for she had given Anna up at birth, and she had been adopted by one of the nurses in the hospital. She brought the baby home and raised her in the large extended family that included Betty Jean and all of Betty Jean's aunts, whom Anna knew as her sisters.

When I spoke to Betty Jean on the phone from my apartment many months before, she told me the same story about Anna's abandonment by Goldie Gadson and subsequent informal adoption, but even as she told it, she hinted that there was more to it—that this was only the official narrative and something else lurked behind the story of Anna's origins, a truth not spoken.

"Now you know how these old people don't like to talk about things," she said. "What they *told us* was that Anna's mother died in childbirth. The midwife carried the baby up the hill to St. Margaret's Hospital. My auntie Alice was working there as a nurse, and she came home and told my grandmother Betty Franklin there was a baby abandoned at the hospital. And that's when they decided to take her home and raise her as their own. I grew up thinking of Anna as my sister. That's how they told it anyhow."

At the time of that conversation, I was too shy to press Betty Jean on what she meant by *what they told us*. As I drove up the I-10 through Mississippi and into Alabama, I had plans to find out more.

I'd done some research before coming to the South. I'd tracked down Anna's 1914 birth certificate from Alabama Vital Records. I'd learned from this document that Anna's birth mother had given her no name. The document says that her mother's name was indeed Goldie Gadson. It states that in 1914

Goldie was a sixteen-year-old schoolgirl. Color: Black. Father: Unknown. Before coming South I had stared at this document many times, looking for clues. I searched the census records from that year, looking for evidence of Goldie Gadson, my supposed great-great-grandmother. The mother's age of sixteen, her occupation "schoolgirl," the sad nameless birth certificate recording this baby born in the "Peacock Track" part of town, suggested to my imagination rape—or at least a child born in shameful circumstances. I wanted to know what those circumstances were, and the relationship of Anna to the family she was adopted into.

It was late. I was tired. I wanted to watch cable television, trawl the Internet, zone out, but I had promised Betty Jean I would call her as soon as I arrived. I assumed she would tell me to come by in the morning—it was past dinnertime—but when she answered the phone, she sounded peppy and indeed told me to come over right then, she was waiting to see me.

She gave me directions, and I left the comfort of the hotel room, dragging myself, exhausted, back into the seat of my rental car. I'd had too much for a few days—too much of my father, too much of the past, too much of the South. As I cruised down Montgomery's desolate and antiseptic main road—past state buildings and the Dexter Avenue Baptist Church where Martin Luther King had gotten his start, where the Student Non-Violent Coordinating Committee had been founded—I wanted nothing more than to be back in my Brooklyn apartment, back in New York.

Since college, I'd always believed California was the opposite of the world I'd grown up in (New England, New York, the northeast coast), but California felt now like an extension of New York and Boston. It was the South that was foreign to me.

Betty Jean answered the door wearing her housedress and slippers and a kerchief over her head. She was small and beaming and brown and lucid. I liked her immediately. She welcomed me into her home—the same house where some fifty years earlier Ann-Lucien Green had returned with my father and his siblings after rescuing them from the orphanage. This was the same house where Anna had been raised after being orphaned herself.

History. My father had history in this home.

And yet I was struck once again—as I followed Betty Jean through a formal sitting room and into a cluttered and warm kitchen in the back—that I didn't quite know the relationship this woman had to my father or to me. Like those Creoles in Jennings, like Ernestine, Betty Jean was acting like we were family, blood, but it was a relationship without an official title. The refrigerator was covered with photographs of family— beaming faces of children and old people, sisters and brothers, cousins and aunts, eighty years of her loved ones. She pointed to one girl and said, "That's Danzi, your cousin." It was Betty Jean's granddaughter, and though her name was spelled differently, she also was named after my father's aunt, Emma Danzy. This was my black family—the proof that I was connected to a large Southern clan who had not married out of the race or fled their origins to escape who they were, who were not tragic or lost. Or at least that's what I wanted to believe, as I settled down in front of the plate of food—macaroni and cheese, cornbread, chicken, a giant glass of sweet tea—that Betty Jean had laid out before me. Everything had the trappings of a reunion, a *Roots*-like return to my lost people, but the fact was, I wasn't even sure these people on South Ripley were my forebears, exactly.

That night in Betty Jean's kitchen, two entirely contradictory stories about Anna's origins emerged.

The first was the narrative I'd been raised to believe, the one involving Anna as an orphan, born one night in the Peacock Track section of town to a sixteen-year-old schoolgirl named Goldie Gadson. This story was clean: the schoolgirl mother died in childbirth and the father was never identified. In this story, Anna, a nameless orphan, was brought into this family of strangers and raised as one of their own.

But in the second story that Betty Jean told me that evening in her kitchen, there was no such person as Goldie Gadson. There was no baby carried by a midwife up a hill to the hospital. That was all a fiction created to protect the reputation of the family. This second story featured the family's pretty sixteen-year-old daughter named Alice. Alice got romantically involved with a young dandy named John Henry Loveless, the son of a wealthy funeral home director and businessman, got pregnant by him, and was sent away somewhere to give birth. Her parents decided to keep the baby and raise her as their own. They must have concocted the story about Goldie Gadson. They named the baby Anna and raised her to believe she was adopted. She grew up telling the world that Alice was her sister.

Which story was the truth and which was the fiction? Betty Jean could not say for certain—she was not yet alive at the time of Anna's birth—but through the osmosis of family secrets, she grew up believing it was the second story, the rumored one.

Betty Jean went into the bedroom and came out with a photograph of my possible great-grandmother, Alice. I was struck silent for a moment by her face. I saw in it, yes, a clear resemblance not only to my grandmother's but also to my brother's features. But maybe that's what I wanted to see. This recognition came after hearing Betty Jean build the case for Alice as my great-grandmother by blood. I stared at the features of this woman with the melancholy eyes, and I saw what I wanted to see, my father's bloodline going back generations, like my mother's.

I asked Betty Jean to describe Alice to me. She said she had been ambitious and brainy, beautiful and striving. She was also not the nicest woman in the world. In fact, Betty Jean said, she was haughty and cold. Still, she was impressive. She grew up to become a nurse, a high-powered position for a black woman at the time. Staunchly independent, she never had any children of her own that she acknowledged, and didn't marry until later in life, to a football coach in Birmingham. He had been warned against marrying her, and it only lasted a few years before "he got out," Betty Jean said with a laugh.

As I stared into Alice's face, I wanted her to be my great-grandmother. But was it true? I asked Betty Jean what she believed.

"I always believed Alice was Anna's mother, but Alice and her sisters, they took their secrets to the grave."

Nevertheless, there were objective facts she told me that evening that seemed to at least buttress this story. Alice was fastidious about her fancy house and didn't like children visiting—except for Anna. Only Anna was allowed to visit Alice whenever she liked.

In fact, Alice took an obvious special interest in Anna throughout her life. She seemed to have her own personal ambitions for Anna; she wanted her to pursue an education the way she herself had, and paid for Anna to go to Xavier University to get her master's degree.

On her deathbed, Alice went into a state of delirium and kept talking obsessively about a phantom "baby under the bed." She left her entire inheritance to Anna (my mother remembers it being in the range of twenty thousand dollars), some of which Anna gave to my parents to put toward the purchase of a house, the house on 1 Robeson Street where I was born.

Betty Jean showed me a letter she'd received from Anna when she was living up north, in Boston, with us. She was in the throes of cancer and wrote of the difficulties in her life:

> Two lumps appeared on the same side where I had the opera-
> tion almost five years ago. They were small but very painful
> beside my upper bowel, ulcers, etc. So before removing the
> lumps I had to go through endless tests. Was in the hospital
> (2) wks my doctor said I should have stayed at least another
> week but if I take it easy at home for at least three or four
> weeks, I should do very well also insisting that I should and
> must eat 7 meals a day to put on the necessary weight I'm lack-
> ing. So much for me—I don't think I shall die soon.
>
> I've plenty to bear in my life time and never wished my
> troubles on anyone but Alice—should have saved her more
> from them. However, I'll keep going until I can't, which keeps
> the mind occupied and that also helps the body.

Betty Jean and I together puzzled over this strange last paragraph, that odd sentence: "I . . . never wished my troubles on anyone but Alice—should have saved her more from them."

We wondered aloud: Why did she wish her troubles on

Alice? Because Alice was her real mother? Because that is what a daughter would wish on a mother who didn't acknowledge her as a daughter?

Betty Jean said she believed Anna knew her whole life that Alice was her mother. The two women traveled together—and Betty Jean thought Alice probably shared this secret with Anna at some point on one of their trips.

But the lie, about Goldie Gadson on the Peacock Track— why would the family create such an elaborate story?

Betty Jean shrugged. "They were Catholics. Recent converts. Maybe they were ashamed."

Before I went back to the hotel, I asked Betty Jean to describe Anna.

She said Anna was "special"—a musical prodigy, highly intelligent, brainy—and a little weird.

"She wasn't like the rest of us. She always had her head in the clouds. But she was real sweet. Real funny and sweet. And she was a genius when it came to music. My mother always told the story about how when Anna was two, she climbed up on the piano stool and started to play. Like she knew how already."

I called my father that night from the hotel to tell him what Betty Jean had said about Alice being Anna's mother.

He was silent for a moment. "That's just gossip. Betty Jean is old. She's just spreading rumors. My mother's mother was Goldie Gadson. She died in childbirth."

There was something else my father had mentioned about his mother once or twice over the years, one of those fragments of his family history he'd offered in passing. He said that while he was growing up, his mother had an affair with an Irish priest.

It was something I had heard but shoved aside. It wasn't that I thought it was an outright lie, exactly, but rather that it was an exaggeration of something insignificant. I mistrusted the source—my father—so I reduced the detail to marginalia in my mind.

Of course now, in retrospect, I can see that this story of the priest had been trailing me all the way to Montgomery. It was there in my father's odd baptismal certificate with the false names. It was there in the little house in Jennings, Louisiana, where we sat around with the family of Creoles whose relationship to us was not clear. It was there, even, in Ernestine Hurston's trailer, where she showed me the yearbook she'd put together for the Zimmer children.

And in a sense it seems the story of Anna and the Catholic priest was there even before my journey South, indeed had always been there, written into the very fabric of my family.

It all came to light on my second day in Montgomery, as I sat in Betty Jean's kitchen eating something called Mexican cornbread and gulping down sweet tea.

Betty Jean had a tiny television propped on her kitchen table, the volume turned down low, and as we talked, her attention shifted back and forth between the talk show on the small screen and me.

I asked her about my grandfather, the Mexican boxer, Francisco José. Had she ever met him?

She laughed. "Mexican boxer? Yeah, I heard that one. But I never met a Mexican boxer. All those years, I never met no Mexican."

I was confused. Anna had made countless trips to Alabama with her three children by Francisco, but he had apparently never accompanied her.

I asked Betty Jean what Anna had told her about Francisco.

She repeated the name as if it were gibberish. "Francisco. Sorry, baby, I don't know much about that."

I continued, "But you must have heard her talk about him over the years. I mean, she had three children with the man. That's where I got my last name, Senna. He left my grandmother and went back over the border, but that was their father."

Betty Jean shrugged. "I only know about Father Ryan."

Father Ryan. I thought of the detail I had buried—the one my father had repeated about his mother, the one I had never taken seriously enough to even wonder about. It was more complicated than disbelief. It had not fit into my image of Anna, had not fit in with any of the other details about her, so I had not incorporated it into my narrative of her life.

But that afternoon in the fading light of Montgomery, Betty

Jean told me a story that not only did not include Francisco José but in which this priest was central.

Father Ryan was, she said, the priest at St. John the Baptist, the church one street over from where we sat. It was the church her whole family had gone to, the church she still attended. "Anna used to play the organ there. She played so beautifully." The affair between Anna and Father Ryan began, Betty Jean believed, the year Anna turned nineteen. Betty Jean couldn't say how but somehow Anna got "into it" with the priest. When Betty Jean's father, Lucien "Buddy" Pierce, found out about the affair, he was enraged. Betty Jean told me she still remembered Anna crying in her room the day Buddy found out. She remembered her mother, Betty Franklin, known to all as Ma' Dear, hovering in the bedroom with Buddy, trying to convince him not to take the shotgun out, not to go shoot Father Ryan, because that was his plan, to go shoot Father Ryan at the church across the road. Betty Jean was just six at the time, but she remembered how everybody in the house was upset, and Anna just hid away in her room, crying. Buddy did not go shoot the priest, but he did *something*, because soon after that night, Father Ryan was sent away to another parish in Louisiana.

Soon after, Anna went away too.

"She followed Father Ryan all over the South," Betty Jean told me, "And then up north. She never came back here to live."

When she'd finished her story, I sat for a while just listening to the hum of the tiny television that sat between us on the kitchen table.

"Was it love?" I finally asked.

Betty Jean smiled. "This was the forties, the South, baby. A black woman with an older white man. You can call it what you want."

I asked her to describe Father Ryan.

She began to rattle off adjectives—"funny, smart, a nice man"—then stopped, stared me in the face, and said: "I just wish he had acknowledged those children."

"Wait a minute," I said. "The priest couldn't be their father—"

Betty Jean scoffed. "Yes, he is. They are all Father Ryan's children."

Back at the Embassy Suites that night, I spoke on the phone to my father, who laughed off Betty Jean's suggestion that he or his sister were the children of Anna's affair with the Irish priest.

"That's ridiculous. No, she's got it all wrong."

But what was the story with Father Ryan? My father had mentioned to me once or twice an affair, but what was the extent of it? And what did he remember about the Mexican boxer?

As he spoke, it struck me that there was still so much I didn't know about my father, so much I'd never thought to ask him.

In the story we'd all grown up believing, Anna was in a jazz band touring the northeast. One night, while playing in Washington, D.C., she met a Mexican boxer who had come to the all-black club with his boxer friends. They married and had three children together. My father had murky memories of living in Spanish Harlem, of Spanish voices, of an apartment tenement, but nothing specifically of the boxer, his father. This last detail bothered me. How would he not remember anything of a man who had fathered three children with his mother? My father was the oldest, so it seemed he would have to remember meeting his Mexican father at some point?

The other story was about Father Francis Ryan, for although my father had no memories of Francisco José, he told me he did remember—all too vividly—the Irish priest. My father confirmed what Betty Jean had told me, that the priest was the main reason for Anna's break with her people in the South: the reason why she had moved north and never looked back.

This priest had been in my father's life for as long as he could remember, a plump, rogue Irish American who kept receding and then reappearing over the years.

According to the official documents I obtained from the Josephite Church in Baltimore, Father Francis Ryan was a priest in Montgomery at St. John the Baptist as part of the Josephite missions to convert colored people into the church.

Later, when my father was an adolescent in the Cabot Street housing projects in Boston, the priest would come to visit them on occasion, sometimes staying a week or two.

On those visits to Anna in Boston, the priest would give my father and his sister money to go out for ice cream and a movie, and when they returned, my father says, his mother would take her time coming to answer the door. She'd be flustered in a housedress and Father Ryan would be visible in the bedroom in his underwear and socks. In the bathroom, after one of these trips to the movies, my father says he found a condom floating in the toilet. He said when he was fourteen he had discovered a drawer full of letters in his mother's bedroom, all letters from Father Ryan. The body of the letters was innocuous—conveying news of people they'd known and daily life in the South. But in the margins of one letter, my father said, Ryan had drawn pornographic doodles and a filthy sexual narrative about what he wished he could do to Anna. There were, he said, stains on the paper that the priest had drawn arrows to, saying they were "prick stains."

"This was at a time when I was being admonished by nuns for having any sexual thoughts," my father said.

According to my father, before Father Ryan would leave to go down south, he would have Anna's children line up before him on their knees so that he could give them his blessing. He made them promise to be good boys and girls.

And yet my father was still adamant at the end of our phone conversation that Father Ryan was not his father, that he was indeed the son of the Mexican boxer.

I persisted: "But don't you think it's strange that your mother could have given birth to three children by this Mexican and none of you remember him? Or that nobody in the South ever met him? That she had a relationship with somebody for that long and it's as if he never existed? The one you remember is Father Ryan. Maybe that means something."

"No, baby, it doesn't mean anything. I was so young that I wouldn't have remembered Francisco before he left. And anyway," he said, "I called Father Ryan in the 1980s, when he was living at a nursing home, just before he died."

"You did?"

"Yeah, I called him and I asked him point-blank if any of us were his children."

So my father had wondered too, enough to call an old man at the edge of death.

"What did he say?"

"He started crying. He said that we weren't his children. That he and my mother had taken precautions. He said he knew it was wrong what he did with my mother, but that he'd felt sorry for her."

"Felt sorry for her?" I let out a little laugh. "A man doesn't sleep with a woman on and off for decades because he feels sorry for her."

My father let out a kind of laugh too. "I know," he said. "I even showed up for his funeral the next year, down in Foxboro. I went and the relatives looked nervous. I introduced myself to them and told them I was the son of Anna Senna, a longtime friend of Father Ryan's."

"Wait a minute. When you called him and he was crying and denying you were his, you believed him?"

"I believed him. Yeah, I never thought it was the case we were his kids. Not really . . ."

His voice petered out and we were both silent then.

When I spoke to my mother the next day, she was as surprised as I was about the extent of Anna's affair with the priest. She had been close to Anna. She likes to say that Anna was her husband during the years she was married to my father. She and Anna took care of the babies together. It was Anna who completed my mother's conversion to Catholicism. And yet Anna had never mentioned the priest. For as close as they were, my mother told me, Anna was the most secretive person she had ever met.

My mother said there must have been love, real love, between Anna and Father Ryan. To have lasted that many years, she said, it must have been a love affair.

My father had a different view, closer in line with Betty Jean's. He said it was a situation of a black woman needing, out of financial desperation, to become the mistress of a white man in power, a story as old as the South itself. My father reminded me of an expression he'd heard growing up in the Jim Crow South: "Scratch a black woman long enough, and you'll find a white man in her past."

The next day I went to visit Anna's alma mater. It was the school she had been attending when her affair with Father Ryan began. Alabama State University was a historically black college in Montgomery not far from Betty Jean's house on South Ripley Street.

Back then, the school was still called State Teachers College. It had been founded in 1867 by nine former slaves and was the first state-supported educational institution for blacks. Betty Jean, thirteen years younger than my grandmother, had gone to college there as well, as had several of her siblings and children. It was an institution with deep roots in our family.

Weeks before, from New York, I had spoken to a woman named Ruby Wooding in the records division of the university and asked if it would be possible for me to see my grandmother's records from when she was a student. She'd said it was possible, but that I had to fax them a letter stating my name and all the necessary information. I had done so.

I went to visit the campus, expecting to retrieve the files on Anna, as I'd been promised. It was a rather sterile campus—rows of gray-brick buildings. Students milled around wearing university sweatshirts and flirting with one another. I found the correct building and was led by a student worker to the office of Ms. Wooding, the woman I'd corresponded with from New York.

A light-skinned woman with a helmet of straightened hair, glasses, and red lipstick, Ms. Wooding didn't smile when the student left me at her door.

"Yes?"

I sensed hostility.

I told her who I was and reminded her of our correspondence.

She blinked at me. "Yes, I remember. I pulled the files."

"So can I see them?"

She shook her head. "No, I'm sorry. That's not going to be possible."

"Excuse me?"

"Those aren't available to the public."

"I'm not the public. I'm the granddaughter."

She then pulled a file with Anna's name on it from a pile on top of her desk. She'd had it ready and waiting for me. She had obviously been planning to hand it over. She opened it, and I could just make out from where I stood a Xerox of a photograph of a dark woman who had to be Anna, though I couldn't see clearly from where I stood.

She looked between the photograph and me and said, "This isn't your grandmother."

"Excuse me? Anna Maria Franklin. Graduated in 1938? Address on South Ripley Street?"

"That's who I'm looking at, but she isn't your grandmother."

I felt slightly dizzy, a tightening in my chest. "Yes, it's my grandmother. I have all of her photographs and files right here in my bag if you'd like to see. I've just been visiting with my aunt, her sister, who lives down the street and went to school here."

Ms. Wooding stared at me coldly through her glasses. "She

doesn't look like your grandmother," she said in a quiet voice. "And I'm sorry, we can't show the files to just anybody."

I tried to sound calm. "Is there somebody else I can speak to about this?"

"I'm the director of records. This is my office," she said.

"Can I at least see the files? I don't have to make copies of them. I just want to look at them."

She shook her head.

"Can I see her photograph?"

She paused. She called out to her student worker. "Make a Xerox of this photograph for the lady. But the file is private. Don't show her the file."

She handed the file to the student, who did as she was told.

I understood quite clearly what was going on. Whether this woman believed I was Anna's granddaughter or not, she didn't like the idea of the two of us being related. She found it offensive. I'd been on the other end of this kind of hostility before; my family, the very existence of us, in all our complexity, was simply offensive to some strangers. The dark grandmother in the photo on Ms. Wooding's desk, the light granddaughter standing before her: it was as if the manifestation of this dissonance had triggered a memory of racial trauma. For how does a complexion change so dramatically in just a few generations? Either through a white man's desire for a black woman or a black man's desire for a white woman. In my case, both.

I left with a small faded Xerox of the photograph of Anna as a young woman, her freshman year in college—the only picture any of us have of her as a young, childless woman. It must have been just before her affair with Father Ryan began. She looks different from any of the photographs I had seen of her since. She is wild-eyed and wild-haired and intense. She is a woman I could imagine getting into an affair with an Irish priest, touring with a jazz band, romancing a Mexican boxer. She is a woman with secrets.

As I drove back to Betty Jean's, I thought about the books on my mother's family I'd seen at the New York Public Library—how excessive was the information out there about them. And what had I of my father's story? A washed-out Xeroxed photo of his mother, which I had to get by begging. Unsubstantiated rumors told to me by a woman who might or might not be my blood relative. Nothing substantive. Nothing preserved under glass.

I told Betty Jean the story of what had happened at her alma mater. She was incensed. She said if her knee wasn't in such pain, she would go over there right now with me and set the record straight. She'd have that woman fired for what she did to me. She called her cousin who had also gone to the school and told her the story of what had happened to me, and together they were incensed on my behalf, which made me feel a little better, though I still had no way of seeing the files and never have.

I spent the rest of the evening sitting once again around Betty Jean's kitchen. We talked about my parents, their difficult marriage, their awful divorce. She told me something that surprised me. She said that she had twice visited Boston while we were living there. I had been very small, too small to remember. She said the first time she came was for Anna's funeral. The second time she came was because my mother had called her, desperate about my father's drinking, and was hoping some of his family could step in and help. Betty Jean and her husband James had flown up to try to talk Carl into getting help, but she said it did no good. "It was bad then, it was so bad for your mother. Carl was in bad shape. We couldn't help. And so we left." She said, "I'm glad to hear your mother is doing well. You tell her to make sure and come visit if she's ever down this way."

My mother never told me that Betty Jean and her husband had flown all the way up to Boston when she needed help.

I wrote her an e-mail later that night asking her about it. She wrote back to tell me that she had indeed called them for help, and they had indeed come up to Boston. She said she had not known them, but she was desperate, and with my father's mother dead, they were the only family elders she knew of to call.

But when Betty Jean and her husband arrived, my mother said, they were decidedly cool toward her. My mother at the time was living on food stamps with us three children and working to support us all. But, she says, she felt that all they could see was her whiteness and privilege.

On the one hand, my mother could not turn to her own family, who would cluck their tongues at my father's behavior as evidence that she had been mistaken to marry a black man in the first place. On the other hand, she could not get help from his remaining family if all they saw was her whiteness, and that useless honor of a name with historical cachet. (As my husband says, "That name and a quarter will get you twelve minutes of parking on Mass Avenue.")

My mother once said to me that if her own father, Mark De-Wolfe Howe, had lived to see her marriage, and if Anna Senna had lived longer, she and my father might have found a way to make the marriage work.

But the two adults who would have been sympathetic to both of them, and who perhaps more importantly would have wanted the marriage to succeed, were dead.

I left Betty Jean—with promises to be in touch—and drove north on the interstate toward Birmingham. I moved toward yet another stranger who claimed to be my relative. I could not say how we were connected, or even if we were. Her name was Yvonne and she had said on the phone from Betty Jean's that she was my cousin. She told me she could help me in my quest if I came and picked her up and brought her back down to Montgomery. She was stranded, she said, without the use of a car. She had a thick Southern accent and said, "I love you," to me before we hung up. I found myself saying, "I love you too."

As I drove, I tried to put a family tree together in my head. My father might be the son of a Mexican boxer named Francisco José. Or he might be the son of an Irish American priest named Francis Ryan. Anna might be the daughter of a schoolgirl named Goldie Gadson, or she might be the secret daughter of Alice, the woman she'd been raised to call her sister, and a man named John Henry Loveless. Despite what the record keeper at Alabama State University believed, I was Anna's granddaughter. But who was my grandfather?

Yvonne lived in an apartment complex called Homewood. I

got lost driving through it, looking for the number of the unit she'd given me, so I called her on my cell phone and she led me through the maze of cul-de-sacs to the right parking lot, where, sure enough, she stood outside talking to me from her cell phone. We waved, acknowledged each other, and yet we kept talking into our phones.

"There you are."

"I found it."

"You look just like your grandmother!"

We kept talking until I was parked and out of the car and just a few steps away from her, at which point we muttered goodbye and hung up and embraced.

She was a thin woman in her sixties with a thick head of straight black hair. Her skin was an ashen shade of dark brown, which she later explained was caused by kidney failure. Her skin, she told me, showing me photos to prove it, was actually a rich warm brown. She wanted me to know what she used to look like, who she used to be before she got sick. The illness made it hard for her to walk faster than a trudge as she led me up the stairs to her apartment.

At the top she paused to catch her breath and apologized to me about the state of her apartment. She explained that years ago, when she was "between homes," she'd had to put her stuff in storage. She'd been unable to pay the rent on the unit for some months, and by the time she got the money together, they had thrown out all her belongings.

Yvonne opened the door and I saw that, yes, she had lost everything. She was living in a mostly empty space. Somebody had donated a couch to her. Somebody had donated pots and pans. But mostly the apartment was empty of the trappings of domestic comfort.

Though I'd driven all this way, I still didn't understand exactly what Yvonne's connection was to Anna, and therefore to me. I asked her as politely as I could.

She laughed. "I'm Veatrice's daughter."

I asked her to explain how Veatrice fit into my tenuous family tree. Veatrice was Alice's sister. "Which makes us cousins," she said brightly, as if it were so simple.

Yvonne brought out a picture of her mother. She had died when Yvonne was only nineteen months old. So Yvonne had grown up motherless, raised by her large extended family. As I listened to Yvonne tell me her story, I thought about luck. When I was young, I hated the idea of luck and all that it suggested: that there were forces in life beyond our control that could make your life easy or hard. It frightened me. But I'd lived long enough now to know that there was such a thing as luck. Yvonne had suffered a lot of bad luck in her life. It had started early with her mother's death when she was just a toddler. But, like Anna, Yvonne too had been ambitious. She'd traveled to Boston and New York, had graduated from college and then law school. She told me that in the seventies she'd gotten into meditation and yoga. She'd been married, had a son. And yet now, here she was in her sixties, nearly homeless, living on Social Security and sick with a potentially fatal kidney disease. Her car had broken down eight months ago and the garage was holding it from her until she could pay the seven hundred dollars to fix the engine. Until then she had to rely on her neighbor, a kindly Egyptian man, to take her to dialysis each week. She paid for the five-dollar cab ride home herself. She was waiting to see if she'd need a kidney transplant in the next year, and she believed that God would rescue her because Jesus loved her.

As she talked, I got the sense that she was completely alone in Birmingham. Her family, Betty Jean and her children, were all living in Montgomery. I asked why she was not living there, where everyone she cared about and who cared about her lived. She said she did want to move back to Montgomery, but she had to get her car fixed first. Everything rested on this car engine getting fixed. She was seven hundred dollars from home.

It was, she told me, the church that kept her going. The church made Birmingham home for her. She invited me to attend the service with her that night. I agreed to go. Tonight I would see, she told me, how she kept going. She only wished it was a Sunday so I could go for the full-length service. But I'd get the picture. She was sure of it.

When I went to pick her up that evening, she had changed clothes and brushed her hair and put on lipstick and was waiting for me in the parking lot. The light was dimming but not yet dark as we drove the winding tree-lined road to the other side of town.

On the drive over, Yvonne spoke to me about her pastor, a woman named Althea whom Yvonne clearly worshipped. Althea had started the church only a few years ago out of the living room of her house. Prior to that she had been a member of another, larger congregation—a church that was getting too crowded for its own good. One day the minister of that church said he'd had a message from God. He was going to pick three people from the congregation to go off and start their own smaller congregations. He stood in front of the parish and spoke the names of three men who he believed had been called by the Lord to lead. When those men stepped up, grinning, to the front of the church, and stood with the pastor in front of the applauding congregation, Althea got out of her seat and walked up there to join them. She told the pastor that she had also had a message from God. He had spoken to her directly to start her own congregation. And she was here to call on anybody who wanted to join her.

The church at first was only a handful of people in her living room. But as the word spread of Althea's power, the audience grew and eventually she rented out a storefront space. Yvonne and I arrived there now and pulled up behind a sparkling white Acura sedan. It was, Yvonne whispered, Althea's car. She'd just arrived too. The car was shimmering. The woman who stepped out from it was shimmering too—tiny, dressed in a flowing black pantsuit, perched on high-heel boots, her hair perfectly coiffed. She was young and brown-skinned and reminded me of the Indian women gurus whose pictures I'd seen on the walls of my mother's New Age friends' homes.

We watched her unlock the church with an entourage crowded behind her and disappear inside, and only then did we get out of the car and follow her.

Inside was a simple white room with rows of folding chairs. Althea stood up in a pulpit, looking down at her audience, chatting with the people who came through the door.

Yvonne and I took a seat toward the front. Yvonne was in her element. People greeted her, hugged her, and I could see that this was what kept her here more than the broken-down car or the money woes. The crowd was almost entirely black except for two white people—a man and a woman—and two Hispanic men.

Before the service began, I went to the back to get a cup of water. The white man was doing the same. He was cheerful and asked me if this was my first time here. I told him I was just visiting from New York. He said he and his sister drove forty miles each week from Tuscaloosa to hear Althea speak. "The pastor's awesome!" he said, and headed back down the aisle to his seat.

The service began with Althea speaking in a subdued voice about her subject for the evening: how to have a passionate relationship with Jesus Christ, our Lord and Savior. The muttering of call and response started almost immediately, a whispering and grunting in the audience, people saying "Amen" and "I love you Jesus." People swaying. There was no music. There was just this small sparkling brown woman talking to this room of people about what it meant to have a passionate relationship with Jesus Christ.

It was a love affair, she said, of the highest order. It was about relinquishing power—about submitting to him, our highest savior. It was about feeling, not thinking. To give yourself over—to not question his love—that was to love passionately.

As she spoke, the audience grew louder, and the room seemed to sway under the energy of her words. Althea began to pace and flail her arms, and her voice grew louder, her words quicker, almost angrier, and then she stepped off the stage and something in the room shifted.

A young man in the front row began to weep. He was thin and dark-skinned, with a shaved head. She approached him and put a hand on his head. "You're crying about your baby. Your baby is very sick. Your baby is in the hospital." The man wept harder and nodded. "My son, my baby son."

She nodded. "You're afraid that baby might die."

"Yes, I'm scared."

"If I were you," Althea said to him, "I would have a conversation with God. I would tell him that I'm giving my son to God right now. I'm giving him up to God. That's what I would do."

The man nodded and fell with a slump into his seat, weeping.

A few rows over, a young woman began to cry and convulse all over, and Althea came to her and touched her forehead and said, "Praise this child," and a group of men raced to stand behind the young woman. She began to babble in tongues, her eyes rolled up into her head, and she fell with a slump into the arms of the men.

They laid her down in the aisle like a corpse.

Althea too began to speak in tongues and moved through the aisles sending audience member after audience member into what seemed to be a trance with just the touch of her hand. Three hours into it, the whole congregation was weeping, half of them on the floor, half of them standing and writhing.

She called all those who had high blood pressure to step down the aisle. A row of overweight women came forward. Althea flailed her arms, and the whole row of them flew backward, as if weightless. They tumbled to the ground in a way that looked like it would hurt, and skirts climbing up around their thighs, they thrashed and moaned as she spoke over them in that secret language that Yvonne whispered to me was straight from the Holy Spirit.

Next she called forward all the people with diabetes, and a larger group—including some of the women from the first group—came forward, and she made a similar gesture over their flailing bodies.

Althea told the whole congregation that she'd decided that each person there tonight could make a wish, quietly, and together they would pray to Jesus Christ to hear that wish.

I closed my eyes and wished to love somebody wholeheartedly, wished for a family of my own, wished for a deep and lasting partnership with a man, something I had not yet been able to accomplish. I worried I was damaged beyond repair, that something had gone so wrong in my childhood it could never be made right.

After we'd made our wishes, Althea walked up to a woman beside me and proclaimed to this woman that she had made a selfish wish. The woman began to wail and nod her head in shame, and when Althea reached out to touch her, she flew backward into the row of chairs behind her, sending them clattering to the ground. She wept on the floor beside me, pounding on her stomach and begging God for forgiveness for having asked for something so selfish.

Althea was standing close to me, and I felt a prickle of discomfort when I realized she was smiling at me. The whole congregation was watching us as she stepped closer to me. She was staring at me so intensely, I blushed and wanted to look away, but I didn't. I could feel Yvonne beside me. Althea said quietly, "And you will know. And you will know." I nodded, hot and dizzy from the four-hour service, dehydrated, half-believing that she had heard my wish. Then she reached her hand out and pushed against my forehead. She said something in tongues. She pushed my forehead again, and a cluster of men gathered behind me, their arms open, for me to fall back.

I didn't faint, but I did close my eyes and go limp, the way I had learned to do in college while rehearsing for civil disobedience. Then I let myself fall backward at Althea's touch, submitting to a state of unknowing. I fell, and the men caught me and held me, dragging me somewhere, I wasn't sure where. They laid me down on a carpet. I kept my body limp and my eyes closed, and a moment later I peeked to see that a crowd of people had gathered in a circle around me. I squeezed my eyes quickly shut, not wanting to disappoint them. I heard their voices as if from a great distance, saying, "Praise Jesus!" and "Save this child." I felt somebody pick up my feet and sway them back and forth in their hands. I wondered if anybody could see up my skirt. I heard Althea's voice saying, "And you will know. And you will know."

All of my worst memories from my childhood revolve around the apartment my father lived in on Cypress Street when I was ten and eleven. I wonder if it is true of everybody's childhood memories: the trauma, no matter how long it went on and in how many different places, localizes around a certain time and place. We return to a singular moment to explain something about ourselves in the present.

My father says the Zimmer Home is where he "got so fucked-up." He locates the damage done to his development there, in those three years, though certainly it began before, and continued after. My memory rushes back always to those two years, when I was on the cusp of no longer being a child. Those were the aftermath years, when the divorce was final, when I had to go after school to my father's apartment and wait for my mother to come pick me up. She was working late and picking up the other two so I would often be sitting in his apartment for hours, either with him or alone.

The trauma was a quiet one, hard to articulate, for I identified with his sadness, instability, and loneliness that suffused the space around me. Something about sitting by that window with my homework, looking out onto the street below, waiting for my mother's car to appear, made me a participant in his moods.

One day after school I walked into my father's apartment and heard voices in his bedroom, laughter. I tried to open the bedroom door, but he stopped me. He told me through a crack in his door that I had to leave. I could see he was naked, and beyond him, a woman in the bed. I fled the apartment, cheeks burning with embarrassment, and walked from Brookline, the town where my father lived, toward Jamaica Plain, the town where my mother lived. It was several miles between these two homes, and it must have been late fall or winter, because midway there, the light began to dim over the city. I found a pay phone at a gas station and called my mother, who was in her office. I asked her to pick me up. She was confused. Why wasn't I waiting at my father's? Why was I out on the street in a strange part of town alone? I told her what had happened and she said she was on her way. I waited for her at a bus depot near the gas station, pretended with a huddle of strangers that I was waiting for a bus too. My mother's car finally pulled up and she brought me home.

That night, my father called and told her he wanted the key back from me to his apartment. I could no longer come and let myself into his home after school. I had to knock and see if he was home, in which case he'd let me in, but if he was not home or did not answer, I would have to wait at a friend's house for my ride home.

I had many friends in the neighborhood around my father's house, but I was too ashamed to tell them that I no longer had keys to my father's apartment, so on the days he wasn't there to let me in, I waited instead in the foyer outside his apartment door.

The pastor laid my feet back down and somebody laid a blanket across my body. And a moment later I could feel that the attention had shifted away from me onto somebody who was weeping at the front of the church. I stayed there on my back and listened to the wailing all around me, the sound of languages that had never existed. I tried to imagine it was an anecdote I might laugh about with my friends, but instead all I could think about was how strange my life was in New York. There I paid a woman I did not know almost a hundred dollars a week for a fifty-minute chance to talk to her about my problems. I sat stiffly across from that woman, accepting her silence as some kind of wisdom. I lived alone in a $1,500-a-month apartment, and I went to yoga each week at a studio where a lithe white girl with a nose ring sat at the front of the room and led us in a Sanskrit chant in a language we did not speak or understand.

This was not so strange, what was happening here in this room.

Here, for free, Yvonne got community and emotion and the sense of being held when much of the time she was so alone. We were all looking for ways to contradict our reality even for an hour, even for four hours.

I heard chairs falling and opened my eyes and saw Yvonne flying off her feet and falling with a crash onto a pile of dead folding chairs. I was concerned for her health, but around her women older and frailer were flying through the air, beating their chests, writhing. I watched as Althea approached two Hispanic men who had until now been standing looking confused and stiff in the midst of all the mayhem. Althea stood in front of them speaking in her tongues, then reached out and touched one of their foreheads. She pushed the man's forehead where she'd touched him, and he dropped into his chair, eyes still open, rubbing his forehead. The other stood, staring at her, dry-eyed and cynical. She pushed his head. He stayed standing. I found myself thinking, "Come on and faint!" She pushed one more time, and this time, the sheer force of her hand on his head made him fall back into his seat, stiffly. He sat watching her, composed, dubious, as she walked away to find somebody who would respond the way she needed him to respond.

I decided I'd been on the ground long enough and crawled on all fours to my seat, where Yvonne was still on the ground, immobile. I tapped her shoulder, and she didn't budge. I was scared. She was elderly, in frail health, with kidney failure and diabetes, lying in an awkward position in a pile of metal chairs. But sure enough a few minutes later Yvonne got up and picked up her chair and sat down, fanning herself with a piece of paper from her purse, and shaking her head, weeping quietly beside me, repeating, "I love you Jesus," over and over again under her breath.

The sermon did eventually end. The Hispanic men left with their heads down, smirking, and I wondered if they had wandered into the service by accident. The rest of the parishioners awoke as if from a long, strange, fitful sleep.

Yvonne accompanied me back down to Montgomery the next day, where she planned to introduce me to a woman who had been a close friend of Anna's during their youth. We were hoping she might be able to tell us something about Alice Parish, John Henry Loveless, and the mystery of my grandmother's origins.

Dessie Redden was in her nineties and lived alone in a small white cottage. When we showed up, she was in the backyard gardening in blue jeans. She invited us inside for soda. We sat in her living room surrounded by memorabilia from the sixties.

Dessie had been a major actor in the civil rights movement. She was a close personal friend of Martin Luther King. She had marched to Mississippi along the Miracle Mile. She and Stokely Carmichael and H. Rap Brown had marched together and set up tents together and been tear-gassed by the state troopers. She showed me news clippings and photographs from that era, clearly the defining moment in her life. She was one of the un-acknowledged legions of female activists of the time.

I asked Dessie, bluntly, what she knew about Anna's origins.

She said she knew the official story, that Anna was supposed to be an orphan from the Peacock Track, but she'd heard rumors all her life that Alice Parish was Anna's real mother. Like Betty Jean, she'd also heard rumors that Anna's father was an under-taker by the name of John Henry Loveless.

"He came from a powerful family. John Henry Loveless's daddy gave money to the city for a school for black children. The son, John Henry, Jr., I don't remember him marrying anybody. He was a sporty kind of something. All the ladies screamed for him. I mean, ladies would fall on their face when he walked by. Anna looked like him, small in stature, medium brown. If you were to look at Anna, you'd say he was her father. And yes, Alice was her mother. Alice was always doing some-thing special for that child. Personally, I didn't like Alice. She ex-pected others to look up to her. See, for her to be an RN was something else. People up in Birmingham were country, and most of her friends looked up to her. But she was mean. We'd all go visit Emma Danzy in Birmingham, and they'd get all dressed up to go to hear Anna play in a recital, and Alice would say, 'You stay here, Dessa.' She made me feel real low and small when I was a child. I never liked her. My second husband lived in Birmingham. He tried to get Coger not to marry Alice because he knew she would boss him around. And he was right. Marriage only lasted a few years." Dessie sucked her teeth, shook her head. "She was no beauty."

The bitterness was still fresh, eighty-odd years later, of the schoolgirl whom Alice had not invited to go to the recital.

I asked Dessie then about Father Ryan. Did she know about Anna's relationship with the priest?

"Sure I knew. Everybody knew," she said. Then, in the next breath, "I always felt bad for those children."

"What do you mean?"

"Not being acknowledged by him. That was wrong."

"You mean my father and his siblings?"

She nodded.

"Those were Father Ryan's children," Dessie said flatly.

"Are you sure?"

"Of course I'm sure."

I looked at Yvonne, who nodded her head in agreement.

"What was their relationship? Were they in love?"

Dessie, tiny and ancient, surrounded by emblems of black history, looked at me, a small sardonic smile playing on her lips. "It was a situation of a white man with a desire for a black woman. Old story. I got felt up by Father McCovey a few times. Ryan was a goody-goody priest in front of the parishioners, then he would have Anna come down to the rectory after the service. But I guess he made it possible for her kids to get what they needed."

Before we left, I asked Dessie if she had any photographs of John Henry Loveless, my potential great-grandfather. All I had to go on were these images of the dead.

"No," she said. "But the school his daddy built is just over there, around the corner. There's probably a photo of his daddy somewhere inside." Dessie said this without pause, the same way Ernestine Hurston had told me without pause, when I called out of the blue, that she'd been looking for my father for the past fifty years.

Dessie sighed. "It's a shame. He built it for black children, but now they've gone and made it a magnet school, and most of the kids there are white. Shame."

The Loveless Academic Magnet School was indeed as close as Dessie had described it. Yvonne and I made our way up the steps and through the front door. Hanging there in the hallway was a portrait of H. H. Loveless, the funeral home director and the father of John Henry Loveless.

The portrait of Loveless was not unlike all those images of my mother's forebears: the stuffed gut and high-collared shirt, the dandyish suit and the manicured hair, the expression of a self-satisfied man staring out at the world. It could have come right out of *The Gentle Americans*, where Helen Howe shares photographs of my white ancestors going back to the May-flower. It could have been one of those faces, only this man was black, and yes, he looked undeniably like my father. Same mouth. Same forehead. It looked almost as if my father were wearing an old-time costume for one of those photo booths at a town fair.

Yvonne saw it too and gasped. "It's Carl," she said.

Later I found reference to the Loveless School in a history book on Montgomery. The history blurb left out any mention that the school's founder had been an affluent black man. It simply said that it was "Montgomery's first junior and senior high school for African American students." The history books made it sound like another charitable institution created by whites for the "unfortunate negro children" of Alabama, like the Zimmer Home.

Yvonne and I stood staring at the portrait for a while, soaking up the resemblance.

I had my camera and wanted to take a photograph of the portrait to show my family, but there was a row of student trophies in the way.

A black security guard was standing nearby, and I asked him if I could move the trophies so I could take a photograph.

He shrugged, said sure.

I told him I believed the man in the portrait was my great-great-grandfather. He looked amused as he began to remove the trophies for us.

As Yvonne and I stood back to take the picture, the school's bell rang, and students emerged from classrooms. They milled around the halls. Every single one was white. The only black faces I saw there in the Loveless Academic Magnet School that day were the security guard's and the portrait of the school's founder and benefactor.

What strikes me as odd is my own surprise, as I dig through their respective family histories, my mother's and my father's. I had never known the extent of the poverty and struggle and trauma of my father's world. And I have been likewise surprised to learn of the privilege and power—the extent of it—in my mother's family.

When I went down south to meet my father's extended family, I learned for the first time that he had come from utter poverty. In the cluttered warmth of Betty Jean's kitchen, listening to her account of the past, with its swirl of motherless and fatherless children, I understood that he had overcome the humblest of origins. Sitting in Ernestine Hurston's trailer, looking at the pictures of the long-lost Zimmer Home, I understood that he had done the near impossible—made something out of nothing, indeed squeezed water out of a rock. Sitting in that shack in Jennings, Louisiana, I understood that he was never supposed to rise above poverty, above his lot as an "unfortunate negro child," the fatherless son of a black mistress to a white Catholic priest. And then I was embarrassed, and a little ashamed, that I had not understood until so late into our lives that he had persevered under such conditions.

I experienced a similar sense of surprise while listening to my mother tell me her family history one day in a Los Angeles café. The information about my parents—both my father's child-hood of poverty and displacement, and my mother's childhood of privilege—had always been there for me to find and to see. But I had never looked. And they never asked me to look. In their marriage—perhaps this is the case with most so-called mixed marriages—they tried to shed their respective origins. They raised us in a state of willful amnesia, in a kind of hard-scrabble bohemian chaos surrounded by artists and intellectuals of varying colors—and in this new world order I was formed. I understood always and already that they were different colors, but my father's family was mysteriously absent, and we were al-ways hovering at the edge of the poverty line, so the fact that my mother's family came from privilege was an abstract concept. How quickly in this country a family can devolve from aristoc-racy to poverty. My mother single-handledly supported us from a series of ill-paying adjunct teaching jobs. She worried about public school quality and restraining orders and food prices and the crime wave in our neighborhood—problems associated with the underclass—while her illustrious middle name, Quincy, sat there like a bad joke.

History was the only inheritance she had. If I wanted to write a book about her family, it would be easy to do. So much of the work has already been done for me.

Her grandfather founded *The Atlantic Monthly*. He was a friend of Henry James. Herman Melville makes an appearance: he was a nephew (by marriage) of my great-great-uncle Captain

James DeWolf—that notorious slave trader. Melville even used his uncle DeWolf as a character in *Moby-Dick*. "Now the Captain DeWolf here alluded to as commanding the ship in question is a New Englander," writes Melville, "who after a long life of unusual adventures as a sea captain, this day resides in the village of Dorchester, near Boston. I have the honor of being a nephew of him."

They were a club. They helped each other out. They married one another and bore one another's children.

I went to the downtown Los Angeles Public Library one day, in a neighborhood populated with the sorriest array of homeless drug addicts I had ever seen, to do a search on my grandfather and great-grandfather. The catalog of books that I found by both Mark Howes on the computer is too long to list. Books by them and about them. The book lineup revealed not only the family tradition of documenting its own accomplishments, but also the way Boston's larger history was intricately woven into the story of my mother's family. The titles included: *Who Lived Here? A Baker's Dozen of Historic New England Houses and Their Occupants. Boston Landmarks. Adventures in Remembrance. Holmes of the Breakfast Table. Representative 20th Century Americans. Later Years of the Saturday Club. Causes and Their Champions. The Atlantic Monthly and Its Makers. Boston: The Place and Its People.* I scrolled down the list, looking up occasionally to glance around at the homeless people who slept at the library tables all around me, embarrassed somehow at the lineage I had stumbled upon.

Afterward I sat down at one of these library tables with a few of my great-grandfather's books. He dedicated one of them— "his big Boston-y book"—to his wife, Fanny Huntington Quincy

Howe, my mother's namesake, with the words: TO FHQH MY
BEST HERITAGE FROM THE CITY OF HER FATHERS.

On that blazing hot August afternoon in downtown Los Angeles, Boston seemed another country. Outside was the flat urban oasis of imported palm trees. Outside was a neighborhood
where *Chinatown* and Charlton Heston's *The Omega Man* had
been filmed. Outside was skid row—human misery and debase-
ment everywhere. I saw a baby stroller being used to tote
around a homeless crack addict's life possessions. I saw a woman
as thin as Karen Carpenter squatting down to defecate in a dry
fountain in broad daylight. I saw an old man lying on the
ground eating crumbs off the sidewalk. The only functional
people were the Mexicans who came every day to shop with
their families. The black people and the white people were similarly afflicted. This was not Raymond Chandler's Los Angeles.
But it was not Boston either. It had no grandfathers on the
brain. I was in the land of amnesiacs.

And yet still, all I'd had to do was walk up to West Fifth
Street and Grand Avenue, to the main branch of the public library, and here it was, at my fingertips once again: my mother's
family history, a record of Wasp accomplishment.

They were writers. All of them. Each generation produced
not just children but books. In the late 1800s one reviewer—
Ferris Greenslet of Houghton Mifflin—chalked this fact up to a
"hereditary birthmark" in my family.

"Family characteristics last a long time in this old town of
crooked streets and politicians," he wrote in reviewing one book
by the family *about* the family. "This book will be . . . of interest, too, for the student of inherited traits."

This side of my family was above all else interested in their own narrative—whether it was of sin or accomplishment. These ancestors never tired of looking into Narcissus' pool. They were invested in remaining the protagonists of the story—and the story was, as far as they told it, a white one. Black people figured into their narratives as backdrop, as in those *Vogue* fashion shoots where the six-foot-tall white woman stands in a throng of Indian peasants, whose darkness and stoutness and primitiveness is there only to accentuate her Western glamour and sophistication. Black people figure into the Howe/DeWolfe/Quincy narratives simply as moral gauges of the white man's psyche. The Howes and DeWolfes believed in the primacy of their own story, and they had unusual access to power and culture compared to most American families, no matter what race. They assumed they were of greatest interest, of importance, to the larger tale of American history.

I have nobody to convince that my mother's history is worth telling. All the groundwork has been laid. Her family's centrality to American history is implicit. I could write a book about them again, and it would surely interest students of "inherited traits." But as I pull down the books and sift through the pages, hundreds of pages, narratives of the DeWolfes, the Howes, the Quincys, the street-sign side of my family, I am overcome with weariness, as if indeed I am being lulled to sleep like my baby to the sound of white noise.

I checked out a lot of books that day at the Los Angeles Public Library, so many I had to go to their gift shop and purchase a tote bag to carry them. On my walk home that day, I saw the strangest thing: a giant beehive, the size of a bed pillow, had formed in the corner of a scaffolding, where hundreds of bees buzzed around it. A homeless woman high on drugs stood a few feet away pointing at it and shaking her head, saying, "That shit is crazy," over and over again. And indeed it did seem crazy that on the edges of skid row a hive would form, nature's symbol of industry and resourcefulness thriving in the urban ruin where no blossoms could be found, nothing could pollinate.

At home that night I tried to read the books about my mother's family but found myself struggling to stay awake. The next day I tried again and once again found those narratives to have a heavy soporific effect on me, the insomniac. After a third try I faced the truth: I was not interested in their overtold story, not the way it had been written by them in the past, at least. In its endless recounting, the story of my white forefathers had become like dead wood, rendering the subjects themselves unknowable.

"It may be the finished monument that completes memory itself, puts a cap on memory-work, and draws a bottom line . . . Only an unfinished memorial process can guarantee the life of memory," writes scholar James Young. And indeed it seemed that all of these books amounted to one obscene monument, and that this bulky edifice served to preserve one official version that became a wall, sealing my white ancestors off from view.

It is, I realize now, my mother's side of the family that is the anomaly. Most people don't have public records and library books to draw upon for their ancestry. Most Americans have an experience closer to my father's regarding their ancestry.

It is his family story in the end that feels more quintessentially American (if we can even locate such a quality). His is a tale as murky as the Louisiana swamp where he'd been born. He is neither a real Southerner nor a real Northerner. He is neither fully black nor fully Mexican nor fully white. He does not know his father; he has only a Mexican surname and a frayed news clipping showing a Mexican pugilist to possibly explain his light skin and mixed features. In the end, my father was only half an orphan—he lived as one for a while, and then was reclaimed by an enigmatic mother. Every descriptive statement you can make about my father can be contradicted by the sentence that follows. He is half of everything and certain of nothing.

Different as their histories are, looking back, I am reminded that my parents' marriage was the product of a context. Theirs was no clichéd sixties interracial marriage, as the Goodman *Boston Sunday Globe* portrait implies, in which my mother took an axe to her father and mother and her heritage by marrying my father. Rather, in a sense, her marriage to my father was an inevitable outcome of her own father's work. And my father, likewise, came not from a monolithic black community but rather from a mother who had broken off from her (already tentative) roots in the Southern black community in her affair with an Irish priest and perhaps her brief union with a Mexican boxer. The fact is, my parents' histories were never as separate as it would seem on the surface.

My mother's father, the Harvard Law professor, never lived to see his daughter marry a black man, but if he had, I have been assured, he would have been delighted to see his Wasp lineage "tainted."

The one photograph of him that sticks in my memory shows a slight, handsome, hawk-nosed man on a sailboat. In another, my mother, a sun-kissed ten-year-old with tousled white-blond hair, stands bare-legged in an oversize striped sailor shirt at the mast, watching her father steer the boat.

As a law professor, his specialty was civil liberties. In the fifties he went before the House Committee on Un-American Activities to defend victims of McCarthyism. He wrote in his book on the constitution: "The greatest brutality of our time is racial inequality."

In his foreword to the first issue of the *Harvard Civil Rights Civil Liberties Law Review*, my grandfather declared his philosophy: "Recent times have reminded us . . . that aspiration, like history, is a seamless web—that when we talk of civil liberties we are discussing civil rights, that when we deal effectively with civil rights we must deal courageously with human misery, that when we take military action with respect to the world around us the achievements that we have sought at home are likely to be postponed."

After his death he was commemorated in an issue of the same journal. Morton Horowitz wrote: "Student idealism forged by the Civil Rights Movement found its faculty mentor in Harvard Law Professor Mark de Wolfe Howe, the advisor to the founding group. In the murderous summer of 1964, Mark Howe joined 125 lawyers who had organized the Lawyers Constitutional Defense Committee as volunteer civil rights attorneys in the Deep South. Until he died prematurely in 1967, Howe devoted himself to the civil rights struggle at the expense of other personal and professional commitments."

Among the materials I've gathered is a newsletter published in August 1965, when my grandfather was in Mississippi. It's called *The County Freedom Train* and was probably one of dozens of such mimeographed newsletters distributed to activists and members of the black community during the dangerous years of change. It covers the minute details of the revolution we only read about in the broadest terms now—the harassment of an elderly black man while he tried to vote, the registration of black children at a white school. "At least 55 students (Negro) registered at Ashland School and 3 registered at Hickory Flat . . . The Negroes of Benton are showing that when they make a stand against segregation, they are serious," reads one entry. "[We know] desegregation promotes cooperation and under-standing as well as it would help to get a better education."

In one of the issues of the newsletter, the anonymous editors write about my grandfather's performance in the courtroom that week. He was at the time defending a group of "Freedom Train" protesters who were being sued for libel damages by a former principal of a segregated school who had been forced to resign because of a boycott against the school.

> Attorneys for the defendants were John Salstonstall, well-known Boston attorney who ran for Congress in 1958, and Mark Howe, a law professor from Harvard and one of the country's leading authorities on constitutional law . . . Mr. Howe stole the show with a brilliant lecture on the right of protest as one of the fundamentals of American democracy. The courtroom was hushed all during his speech, and the only disappointing thing was that he didn't speak longer. After the trial, one white man was heard to say, "I don't give a damn about those lawyers, but they sure know their business." . . . Re-ferring to Howe, Negroes said such things as, "He's a good un,'" and "Man, he is beautiful." Many have asked for the addresses of the lawyers since they gave us their services free of charge and plan to carry the case to the supreme court if necessary.

My grandfather died in 1967 of a heart attack. That June the *Harvard Law Review* published a cover story honoring his legacy, "Mark Howe: In Memoriam." The author was his colleague at Harvard Law School, Paul A. Freund. At one point he reminisced: "The question was once raised [to Mark Howe] why so many Negroes hold white men in contempt . . . and Howe's answer was, 'Because they know we are cowards.' "

Just before he dropped dead that year, at the age of sixty-one, my grandfather convinced my mother to go south and work for CORE. She did what her father told her to do. She went as a writer to report on the atmosphere in Selma and Montgomery, Alabama. When she returned, she continued to work in Boston for CORE, doing housing violation reports—trying to bring cases against slumlords.

Though she was politically active, she was also beginning her career as a writer. It was during this time that she published her first novel, *Forty Whacks*, and soon afterward a book of poems, *Eggs*. She started a literary magazine called *Fire Exit* with her friend the poet Bill Corbett.

Soon after her father's death, she mentioned to a friend that she needed submissions for her new issue of *Fire Exit*, and he mentioned having met a young black writer he thought was very gifted. He told her the name, and she heard "Carol" rather than "Carl" and for a moment thought it was a woman. But then her friend clarified: "Watch out you don't fall in love with him."

"He said it because Carl was so good looking," my mother tells me now.

She requested work from this young gifted black writer, and he sent her some stories. The stories were excellent, and she called him to discuss them. She was living at home at the time, helping her mother prepare to move back to Ireland after her father's death. She invited Carl Senna to her house to talk about the story. He arrived in a taxicab in a pinstriped suit, smoking a cigarillo. She thought he was "the most handsome thing she'd ever seen."

They were immediate friends and spent their time together talking about writing and books. By the end of that first meeting he had borrowed ten dollars for his cab ride home.

My father's short story "Chill Morning" was published in *Fire Exit*. It is semi-autobiographical. The protagonist, Ramon, has a younger brother, Jose, who, along with a friend, plans to rob and burn down the store of a "price-gouging" Ukrainian Jew who has stiffed the black community. Ramon goes along with the crime only because he is "so worried . . . for my brother's danger." His heart is not in what they do, but once inside the store, he taps into his own rage at the store owner and the racist city around them and goes along with the crime, even shooting the cash register. Afterward the three men go back to Ramon's apartment, and Ramon gets high and watches the gloomy northeastern city beyond the window. Ramon recalls his childhood mornings in Louisiana. "Far away long ago, outside the stony cold cluster of buildings, bland colors and poisonous air of the East, in Louisiana, a town of quietness, fresh air and vigorous life, the twittering of leaves in miles and miles of bayous and country plain." The mother in the story figures as a beloved, gentle figure who Ramon is afraid will be hurt by their actions. It is this mother who moved the boys from their beloved Louisiana to the harsh North, and in a stream of consciousness Ramon recalls Irish nuns, Latin prayers, and harsh Catholic pieties. *"Mother, I cannot take it . . . Let me go somewhere else, to the public schools . . . Why can't we go back South, home . . . It hurts, Mother, they made me feel so bad . . . Shh, wipe your tears, It'll be okay. Don't pay them any attention. Just do your work, for me dear. And pray.*"

My father was the ultimate other to my mother—in terms of class, in terms of race, and perhaps in the end most profoundly, in terms of religion. His childhood had been steeped in religion, whereas her parents had administered a heavy dose of atheism and irony.

It was months after the story came out that they became romantically involved. "We were both scared of each other," my mother says now. "It was a huge divide. I was older, whiter, richer."

My mother had dropped out of Stanford, had been briefly married to and divorced from a conservative white biologist she met in college, had joined Andy Warhol's Factory, and lived on the Bowery in New York, where a local newspaper voted her "slum goddess of the Lower East Side." So in many ways she was worldlier than my father.

My father was four years younger than she was and a student at Boston University. He worked part-time as an orderly at a mental hospital. The apartment he lived in was, she says, "extremely grim." There were prostitutes living in the building. On the door to my father's apartment his name was written "Carlos Francisco José Senna," playing up his connection to his missing Mexican father.

My mother remembers that my father at that time was obsessed with several ideas. He said that married women were equivalent to prostitutes. He thought many white people he met were actually black people passing as white. He was obsessed with the idea that black music was coded and that white people would never understand it.

The first time my mother visited his apartment on Massachusetts Avenue near Symphony Hall, his mother showed up while they were there. She had come over to clean his place. My mother recalls being struck by this fact—a mother coming over to clean her grown son's apartment. His mother still lived in the Cabot Street projects in Roxbury, where my father had come of age. My mother remembers Anna being kind and Southern and quiet.

The first night my parents became romantically involved, my mother says they were both nervous and frightened by the encounter. It was almost as if they were being told to kiss by somebody else, she says. She describes that first embrace as if it were a cold, almost mechanical occurrence, as if they were two puppets being moved into each other's arms by forces of social change rather than two individuals falling into love or lust. "It wasn't passionate," she says. "It was unsettling."

My mother's father was dead. Her mother had moved back to Ireland. She felt in some ways like an orphan. She was in many other ways lost. Soon after my father and she got involved, she went to California to visit her sister. Her friend, the poet Robert Lowell, was in California at the time following the Eugene McCarthy campaign. She went to visit him in Los Angeles at McCarthy campaign headquarters, the same night Bobby Kennedy was shot. She spent the night watching the news with a phalanx of devastated McCarthy supporters in a downtown hotel next door to the hotel where Kennedy had been shot.

My father at the time was in New Mexico doing political organizing for a Chicano group. The way my mother tells it, it was as if the Kennedy assassination propelled them into each other's arms. She decided to go join my father there, in

New Mexico. It was there, under the Sante Fe sun, far from the Deep South and the Deep North, that they decided to get married.

"We were both so lost. We decided to get married. And immediately our luck changed."

My mother was walking through Harvard Square one day when she bumped into a man from Tufts who had just read her first book, *Forty Whacks.* He hired her on the spot for a job at Tufts. He mentioned as they spoke that they were also looking for somebody who could teach black literature, and she mentioned my father, and they hired him too. At the same time my father was hired to be an editor at Beacon Press.

My mother explained to me once that their attraction to each other was intellectual. "We liked to talk to each other," she said. "He was outstandingly intelligent. He always had a new angle on things. He saw the world both through literature and through bitter experience. He was remarkably well read for somebody of our generation. He was unashamed of liking and knowing William Blake as well as the Communist Manifesto. I was drawn to his intellect. We always had something to say to each other. It was an endless conversation. Never boring, but endless."

People remembered them as a couple, decades later. Together they made a strong impression—complicated, difficult, but an impression nonetheless. I once came upon an interview, in a small poetry journal called *Crazyhorse*, with the poet Robert Creeley, who had been a friend of theirs in the sixties and seventies when he lived in New Mexico. The interviewer asks him what contemporary poets he likes to read, and he mentions my mother—and then goes on a tangent about meeting both of my parents together at the start of their relationship.

[Fanny Howe] was married for a real time to an extraordinary person, Carl Senna . . . I remember once they came to see us in New Mexico. Carl asked me to introduce him to the black revolutionary element of Albuquerque, New Mexico. Which is very small. In New Mexico, if you're black, you're an Anglo. To the Chicanos, you're part of the Anglo culture. So if you want to be black and white, go to New Mexico. So in any case, he was really terrific. On the one hand a very charming, very attractive, very bright man, but boy was he ever—not irresponsible, just sort of careless and footloose as the husband, so that Fanny's real rapport is with his mother with whom she forms a very particular relation, because you know Fanny comes from Boston Brahmin . . . John Quincy Adams stuff.

Not long ago I met a woman, a poet and scholar, about the same age as my mother. She recalled meeting my newly wed parents in the late sixties at a dinner party in Cambridge. She told me her impressions of them: they were radical, and looked down on the other dinner guests, who were not radical enough. And this too: "It was obvious they adored each other."

As a young couple, my parents were the inspiration for *The Professor's Daughter*, a literary thriller by British novelist Piers Paul Read published in 1971. The author befriended my parents in 1969, a year he spent living in the United States, and apparently they sparked his imagination. He turned my father into a racially ambiguous Harvard student from New Mexico and added an over-the-top sixties plot. The novel is described on the book jacket as being about "a daughter of a high-powered Harvard professor who gets involved with one of her father's political students and with a plot to assassinate the local senator who also happens to be her mother's lover."

In real life, my parents were married in October 1968 in their home, a former Episcopal church turned into a house on Warren Street in Boston's South End. The black Baptist minister, Rev. Michael Haynes of the Twelfth Street Baptist Church in Roxbury, performed the ceremony. My father wore a Nehru jacket—popularized in the States by the Beatles—and my mother wore a gold lamé minidress. Afterward a reception was held at their friends' house in the South End brownstone. It was a raucous party that went on till morning. All my parents' worlds came together: the old-money Wasp elite, poets and bohemians, Boston literati, the Harvard Law School crowd—colleagues of my grandfather—the *Atlantic Monthly* crowd, some of my father's friends from Roxbury, and my mother's aunt, Helen Howe, author of *The Gentle Americans*. Her uncle, Quincy Howe, a well-known newscaster on *CBS Weekend News* and a contemporary of Edward R. Murrow, came from New York City. Quincy Howe had moderated the 1960 debate between Nixon and Kennedy and was unapologetically leftist. He hit it off that night with my father's mother, Anna, who was still living in the Cabot Street housing projects in Roxbury. Quincy Howe, son of Boston's Beacon Hill elite, and Anna Senna, orphaned daughter of Alabama, danced together, one song after another, late into the evening.

More fragments:

Walking into my mother's house one day in 1994, during the O. J. Simpson trial, hearing her in the kitchen talking to somebody on the phone in an intimate, chatty tone about the trial. She was laughing, agreeing with this somebody about an ironic twist they'd both noticed. When she hung up the phone and emerged from the room, I asked whom she was talking to. "Oh, your father," she said matter-of-factly. "We were talking about the trial." My feeling of dismay.

The two framed portraits hanging in my mother's kitchen while I was growing up: one of Dr. Martin Luther King, Jr., head down, pensive, in thought, the other of President John F. Kennedy, head down, pensive. Once, when I was very small, I pointed at the photographs and informed a visitor that King was my father and that Kennedy was my grandfather.

A dream I had once. It was late fall in New England and my mother and I were on a boat, crossing the water to her home on Martha's Vineyard. It was nighttime, cold outside, the end of the tourist season, and as we stood staring out into the darkness, my mother told me she was frightened to spend another winter alone on the island in that big old house. She was facing old age and didn't want to live it out in solitude on that island. I sensed that she wanted me to come live with her, to be her companion, and there was an old tug of mine to return to her, the womb, the daughter-mother bond, safety from the world. I knew it was impossible. I had already left that home and I could never return. Still, I was worried about her. And in the dream, I asked if she had any friends who might want to come live with her, any old friends who were in a similar predicament. She paused and said, "Well, there is one." "Who?" I asked. "Your father," she said. My thrill, in the dream, thinking this was the obvious solution. They would grow old together, take care of each other, these two who had together brought three children into the world. Waking up from the dream, recognizing its absurdity, falling back to sleep, a dreamless one this time.

My father calling me one Sunday, over and over again until I finally picked up. Telling me the same joke about Al Sharpton over and over again until I relented and laughed.

Him calling me another time and going on and on about somebody we both knew, a rant about how this person had betrayed him, me rolling my eyes on the other end of the phone, him stopping his rambling to say, "What else about me irritates you?" Me, blushing, caught.

The look on his face after his first trip to the Middle East— a kind of joy and wonderment and freedom I had never seen on his face before.

His taking us to the museum when I was a child—to the Egyptian exhibit, in particular, pointing around at the room full of ancient artifacts and telling us that this was Africa too.

In honor of this fact, naming our dog Anubis. Having to give the dog away because it snapped at children.

The time after one of his trips to Egypt when he arrived to pick me up wearing a floor-length white dishdasha and a *shora* on his head. I was staying with my white grandmother in Cambridge and I remember laughing as I watched him come down the hallway of her building in his costume. He wore a sideways smile, a hint of irony in his eyes, as if there were two of him: the one inhabiting his body, and the one watching this body perform from somewhere beyond the periphery of his skin.

His favorite joke from the Jim Crow–era South: "If a black man wants to sit at the front of the bus, he just puts on a turban."

The way he used to, for many years, write letters to editors of major newspapers—commentaries about politics—under a pseudonym. The name, he explained to me once, belonged to a boy he'd known when he was just a high school student, a black boy who was the first genius he'd ever known, light years ahead of any of the white kids in their class, a young prodigy whom he had befriended. He told me he didn't know what had happened to the boy, whether he ever fulfilled his promise, but for years my father borrowed his name whenever he wanted to say something important in print. It was as if he was trying, through identity theft, to pay homage to this lost friend of his youth—or maybe he could not quite embrace the fact of his own genius.

There is a true story about my father and me that I've been trying to turn into fiction for years. I've written drafts of short stories that are versions of this tale, but hard as I try, I am never satisfied with the results. Perhaps I am too attached to the real story, unwilling to depart from the truth of what happened in order to turn it into satisfying fiction. Perhaps I am too afraid of transforming the details, somehow resistant to getting that necessary distance, afraid the real will be swallowed into the imagined. Or perhaps it is because what I am remembering is already fiction, the way all memories become fiction over time.

The story itself involves a preposterous lie. It was the only time I can remember when I, as a child, went off to do anything alone with my father. My father had received a piece of junk mail, a letter from a time-share resort company informing him that he was the lucky winner of one of three prizes: a sports car, a movie camera, or a knife set. The prizes were a lure, of course. The letter stated that in order to claim his prize, he had to visit the time-share headquarters in New Hampshire and go on a tour of the model property there. The letter stipulated that it was an invitation only for married couples. No singles or students. And furthermore, married couples had to tour the property together. My father called and told us about the prizes—he knew he wouldn't get the car, but maybe we'd get one of the other things. We kids wanted that movie camera and begged him to go claim it for us. But he needed a wife. And my mother wasn't interested in playing that part.

Somehow—I'm not sure how the discussions went—we all decided that I would go and pretend to be his wife. I was at the time twelve years old and a decidedly androgynous kid: flat chest, mushroom-cut hairstyle, more interested in horses than boys.

The day of our big date came, and my sister did my makeup while I sat wearing one of my great-aunt Helen's silk blouses from the trunk of old clothes we'd inherited from her. My sister went overboard. She smeared on foundation, rouge, mascara, eye shadow, and fuchsia lipstick. She teased my hair, hoping to make me look less prepubescent. She put me in a giant coat and put one of my mother's wide-brimmed straw summer hats on my head, still hoping to disguise the fact that I was twelve.

I looked like a twelve-year-old truck-stop whore.

My father beeped from outside.

He looked at me slightly askance when I approached his car. I felt anxious as I got into the passenger seat. I wasn't used to being alone with him—my sister and brother were always with me, cushioning me on both sides. Being the middle child, I was swallowed by them, protected by them—disappeared among an adorable brother on the one side and a beautiful and gifted older sister who was my father's undisputed favorite by leaps and bounds on the other.

Now, he and I, husband and wife, drove north out of Boston

toward the time-share resort. My father drove with his head cocked to the side in thought, his arm slung over the back of my seat, listening to the news on the radio. He seemed as uncomfortable alone with me as I was with him.

He kept glancing at me, troubled, it seemed, by what he saw. He asked me a few questions about school, and as I spoke, he interrupted me. "It's your voice," he said. "That's the giveaway. You talk like a kid. They'll figure it out only if you speak."

"So I shouldn't speak?" I said.

"Yeah, you shouldn't speak."

He was quiet then, thinking, his eyes on the stretch of interstate ahead. He looked back at me after a moment.

"I've got it. You don't speak English. You don't speak a word of English. That's why you can't talk. That's why you're so quiet." He nodded his head. "We're Puerto Rican." He chuckled. "We're from Ponce de León. You're my child bride. I'm a Puerto Rican who went home and married a twelve-year-old kid." He began to laugh. "And you barely speak a word of English. I'm your new husband, and you don't speak a lick of English." He was laughing now, and so was I, at the sick ingenuity of it. "Just keep your clap shut, and let me do the talking."

For the rest of the drive he practiced speaking in a Spanish accent. It was terrible, sounded Slavic at its best, Mandarin at its worst. He didn't speak any Spanish, but he tried to pepper his speech with common phrases that had been swallowed up into the larger American culture. *Hola. Sí, sí. Taco. Burrito. Enchilada. Puerto Vallarta.* He'd never been to Puerto Rico, but he liked the name of the town he'd heard of. Ponce de León. He pronounced it *Pon-say-dee-lee-own.*

As we drove, a manic excitement gathered in the car. Behind my nervousness was excitement. I was leaving the world of relative safety behind, my mother's world, for something dangerous. I was twelve and didn't understand the full twisted nature of our pantomime, me dressing as my father's child bride, but I understood in some ineffable way that we were breaking the law.

Our tour guide at the New Hampshire resort headquarters was a thirty-something white woman in a beige business suit who did a double-take when my father—in his mangled Spanish accent—introduced me to her as his wife. She blushed and laughed and coughed and said more than once, "Your wife is so young, Mr. Senna!" as she drove us slowly around the property in a silver sedan.

My father sat beside her in the passenger's seat, I sat in the backseat, sweltering in my overcoat and wide-brimmed hat and the silk clothes and makeup. She glanced at me in the rearview mirror from time to time as she went on and on in a memorized monotone spiel about the benefits of going time-share.

"So you see, Mr. Senna, it allows men like yourself and your wife to stay at some of the world's finest resort properties and luxury condos without having to buy the property or pay expensive resort rentals."

My father nodded, impatient to get to the gifts. "*Sí, sí,* sounds very—nice? Eez that the word? Nice?" His accent had deteriorated, and he moved in and out of having one and not having one.

The woman said at one point, "Your wife is so quiet, Mr. Senna."

"She speaks no English," he told the woman. "She just moved here from Puerto Rico."

The woman eyed me where I sat drenched in sweat. I could

glimpse my own face beside hers in the rearview mirror. My makeup had smudged, I had raccoon circles around my eyes. The foundation my sister had applied was too light and too orange for my skin. I was hot, but I was afraid to take off my coat for fear she would see my stick-thin, clearly prepubescent body. I tried to open the window, but the tour guide had enabled the childproof lock so it wouldn't go down.

"How old is she exactly?" the woman asked, as we pulled up in front of the mock-up property.

"Eighteen," my father said, climbing out of the car. "Legal."

He stood with his chest puffed out, arms akimbo, surveying the property like he was really considering buying it.

In the end, when the tour was over, the woman told us we had a choice of the two bottom-cheapest gifts: the knife set or the movie camera.

"No car, huh?" my father said. "I thought we were getting a car out of this."

The woman apologized that we weren't getting the car. She then suggested to him, in a conspiratorial voice, that between the two remaining gift choices, we choose the knife set.

I had not said a word in the entire hour of wandering the property. I had not spoken a yes or a no, had remained entirely silent. But now I blurted out, in perfect English, "You said we were getting the movie camera."

"Shhh," my father said, cutting his eyes at me.

The woman blinked at me, nonplussed, and it struck me that she had not believed we were Spanish-speakers, had maybe not believed we were married, from the start.

"Trust me, get the knife set," she said. "Honestly? We've had some complaints about the movie camera."

But I wanted the movie camera. I had headed off that day promising my brother and sister I'd come back with a movie camera. I said it again, "You promised the movie camera."

"Whatever you say," the woman said with a sigh. This time she directed her words at me. She was sick of us. She knew we were lying, and she wanted us gone. She worked on commission. This had been a waste of her day. She stomped off to the stockroom to fetch our free gift.

We kept straight faces until we were off the property and heading south on the freeway. Then my father began to speak in his mangled Puerto Rican accent, recounting the details of our scam. I told it back to him. It was history already, lore. *Boy had we pulled one over on that stupid woman*, I said. *Boy, did she look shocked to learn I was his wife. Boy, did his Spanish accent suck.* We laughed so hard that at one point my father started to get an asthma attack and had to pull over on the side of the road, and that only made us laugh harder. I couldn't breathe myself. It was that funny. And it was ours—our father-daughter experience. In my lap I held our prize: the generic white box with the movie camera inside. Over the course of the next week, my mother and my father both separately tried to make the camera work, but it would not even turn on. Eventually we threw the thing out.

M y husband came to me in the heat of August. He came from out west to save me, it seemed, from the debris of Brooklyn. He had come to airlift me to safety, sanity, a wider sky and a wider future. After years surrounded by effete New Yorkers, men I could beat at arm wrestling, he seemed to me to be the last of the real men—dirt under his nails, a sense of chivalry. He was a man who could fix things. He spent three days in my fourth-floor walkup, in ninety-eight-degree weather sans air conditioning, helping me put my life into boxes. We were only a few months into our relationship, and I thought, watching him tape up one more box of college books: *This could kill us. It's too early for this kind of drudgery. He's supposed to see me at my best, bikini-waxed and smelling pretty. He's not supposed to be cleaning out the filth in my closet.*

But we did it. Many giant garbage bags were in order. I'd been living like a graduate student for too long—futon couch, milk crates as night tables.

On our final night in Brooklyn I faced the clothes problem—ten years of impulse buys stuffed into my closet. Tomorrow the movers would come to take what remained of my belongings into Manhattan Mini Storage, and this man and I would get in my car and begin our drive west, toward Big Sky Country. Tonight I vowed to be ruthless. I would throw out anything I had not worn in the past year. So out the clothes went. We put them in heavy black trash bags and lugged them down to the street. As we did it, an old homeless man caught on to what we were doing. We nicknamed him Mr. Bojangles because of the way he dressed, in a rumpled Charlie Chaplin suit and tie. He pushed a grocery cart and came in shifts to crawl over those bags, looting what he wanted, throwing the rest of it onto the street.

It was getting late. A whole rack of maybes remained in my closet. The black knee-high boots with the scuffed heels I thought I might need again, though they were agony on my bunions. The silver floor-length dress I'd worn at my twenty-sixth birthday party and had not worn since.

And the brown shearling coat from my father.

I'd been wanting a shearling coat for as long as I could remember, but when my father finally bought me one, it wasn't exactly the style I'd coveted. He'd gotten it wrong. He brought it down to me from his home in Canada. I rarely wore it unless the temperature plummeted. It was too large, and the boxy cut didn't flatter me.

Earlier, before I started packing, I had vowed to be ruthless.

Now I pulled out the shearling coat and held it up between us.

"What about this? I should keep this, right? It's from my father—"

"Have you worn it in the past year?" he asked.

"No, but it was a gift—"

"Will you wear it in California?"

"No—but . . ."

"Sounds like it should go to Mr. Bojangles. Along with the rest."

I nodded. It was sensible. This was exactly the kind of clear-headed answer I'd made him promise to give me. I stuffed it into the garbage bag and thought: *This will keep Mr. Bojangles warm for many a winter to come.*

We carried the last of the bags out into the darkness and left them in a pile on top of the others, most of which had already been ransacked. Two days earlier it had seemed impossible we would ever clear out my life, but we were finished. The apartment was devoid of anything the movers weren't taking to storage in the morning. It was time for food.

We ordered takeout and sat on the floor in the sweltering heat, clutching our chopsticks, surrounded by bare walls and stacks of boxes and rolls of tape, too exhausted even to eat much, both of us stunned that we were actually finished. The closets were empty. The cupboards were bare.

After we ate, my husband-to-be examined a map and spoke about the drive ahead, the route we would take, how long he thought it would take us to get to Montana. I half listened. My mind was not with the trip. It was on the sidewalk below, where Mr. Bojangles would soon return to claim his loot—and the shearling coat my father had given to me. As I thought of the coat I was discarding, a panic grew inside me. It grew, like a twister gathering speed in my chest, until without warning I jumped up and said that I'd made a terrible mistake in throwing out the coat. I needed to go down and get it from the garbage before Mr. Bojangles came to take it from me. There was an edge to my voice.

"But I thought you said you hadn't worn it in years—"

"I haven't. But I might, someday. And it was a gift, like I said, from my father." I was speaking too fast. And then I was down the stairs, heading out into the soupy night air. Mr. Bojangles had not returned yet for his next load. And so, like him, like a homeless scavenger, I climbed on top of the mountain of bags, opening each one, and digging inside for the one that held the shearling coat. I finally found it toward the bottom of a bag, pulled it out, carried it with me upstairs.

"I'm sorry," I said, dusting it off. "It's stupid. I just—I don't know. I can't do it. I need to hold on to it."

And then I was crying. I had told him only the briefest details of my troubled relationship with my father, but now, standing before me, he didn't ask why I was crying. He just held me. "It's okay to keep the coat," he said. "That's fine."

And here it is, years later, still sitting in storage—a coat of potential. Perhaps someday, I think, it will keep me warm. Perhaps someday I will grow into a woman the coat will fit—or the coat will transform into the perfect gift I've been waiting to receive.

There was one more secret about Anna that I had yet to discover. It came to me when I thought I had nowhere further to go in uncovering the story of my father's family history. I had begun the research into my grandmother's life in New York City, when I was single and childless, and thought I had finally finished it years later, married and with child on the opposite coast. In the course of my quest, I had been propelled, it seemed, into another world altogether.

One day I received an e-mail at my home in Los Angeles. It came from a genealogist who said she was doing research on my family name, "Senna."

"The family connection," she wrote, "would be through Anna (Franklin) Senna, who was the daughter of Goldie and Thomas Franklin. My research indicates that she was born in Alabama." The woman asked me to please help her connect with my father, Carl, whom she had been trying to track down.

The language in her letter struck me as intentionally vague. It did not reveal why she was interested in our family name—or what, if anything, connected her to our family. It was strange that she had mentioned the name Goldie—and who was this

Thomas Franklin she was referring to? And how did she know my father was Carl, and why was she so eager to contact him? It seemed too odd a coincidence to me, furthermore, that a genealogist should write me when I was at the end of researching my grandmother for this book.

In any case, I sent her my father's e-mail address.

When I next spoke to him, he had already been in touch with the genealogist, who, he informed me, was actually an "adoption reunion specialist." She had been trying to contact my father to tell him he had a long-lost sister, a woman whose first name was the feminized version of his own. Carla Latty had strong reason to believe she was the daughter of my grandmother, Anna Franklin—and therefore was my father's sister.

The facts were these: Carla Latty had been born in 1952 and given the name Bernadette Senna by her biological mother. Sometime soon after her birth, she was placed as an infant in the New York Foundling Hospital. According to the papers she had gotten from the home, her father was reported by her birth mother to be an Irishman, five feet seven inches tall. Her mother was described as a black woman from Alabama who had three other children, at the time in foster care. Their ages matched those of my father and his siblings.

A few days after Carla contacted my father and me for the first time, I woke at dawn beside my husband and something floated into my mind, a memory of a letter I had received eight years earlier and had not thought of since.

It had been 1998. The letter had come to me one day, a slim white envelope addressed to me. The note inside was handwritten on two sides of a plain sheet of paper.

"I am writing in efforts to locate my birth mother," it read. "I have searched for her for many years but have been unsuccessful so far. Thanks to advances in computer technology, I came upon your name, which closely matches the information given to me by the adoption agency that put me up for adoption."

I remember thinking the letter from 1998 was a hoax because when I turned it over to read the other side I learned that the author of the letter had been born many years before I was born. Clearly I wasn't her birth mother.

Anna Maria Senna.

Danzy Maria Senna.

I never thought the author of the letter might be searching for my grandmother. I never thought about the fact that my name is almost hers. I simply noted the author's error and put the letter aside. I never did reply.

In the weeks that followed Carla's first correspondence with my father, she told him her story, which he related, with some skepticism, to me. Anna, while living in New York, had given birth to a baby girl fathered by a white man. She had named the baby Bernadette Senna and placed her in the Foundling Hospital. Carla had been born in September of 1952, during the period when my father and his siblings were still living in the orphanage in Prichard, Alabama, just before they were rescued from there by relatives.

Anna once had confided in my mother that she had suffered a nervous breakdown while living in New York City. She said she had been committed for a period to a mental hospital there. Another time, Anna said something out of character, an outburst about a priest they knew whom my mother had said she was going to approach for marital advice. "Priests know nothing about marriage," Anna said with uncharacteristic sharpness.

These details came back to me now, in light of Carla's appearance. I wondered if this period in New York when Anna had suffered a breakdown had been the time she'd given birth to the baby girl the nuns called Bernadette, the product of her relationship with her priest. I tried to imagine Anna at this time, far away from her three older children, knowing they were stuck in an orphanage. I tried to imagine the decision she'd made— coldly? agonizingly?—to give this fourth child away. Was the decision so painful—the culmination, one assumes, of a lifetime of painful moments and decisions—that it sent her into such despair she had to be hospitalized?

My father was suspicious. He thought Carla was possibly lying, more likely confused. Still, he agreed to meet her in New York to find out more, and I made plans to join them both there.

Carla organized our meeting for lunchtime in a Baruch College conference room. She explained that her girlfriend, known as Sugar, was an administrator at Baruch and would be present for our meeting. My father, in Boston the night before, promised he would leave for New York at the crack of dawn so that he would get to town with hours to spare. I arrived at the appointed time but my father was nowhere to be found.

I called Carla's cell phone from outside the building, and she and Sugar came out a few minutes later to meet me on the sidewalk. Carla was small, with skin the same light brown shade as my father's and short dark hair. I didn't immediately see a resemblance to anybody I knew. Her girlfriend, Sugar, was Indian, and wore a bright, flamboyant sari, her short hair streaked white with Susan Sontag ferocity.

We all embraced, awkwardly. It was not the first time I'd met relatives of my father's I wasn't sure were really relatives.

I followed them inside, and we sat around the conference table with sandwiches provided by Sugar.

I told the two women my father would be in later, but I could see from their smiles that they didn't understand just how late. They served me lunch, and as we sat there, waiting for my father to show, Carla told me her story.

She had grown up believing she was the biological child of her parents, Ernest and Regina Latty.

Her father, Ernest, worked as a police detective in New York City; Regina was a housewife. Ernest's family roots went back to Jamaica and the Virgin Islands, while Regina was a classic American mix of black and Irish and Native American. She'd been raised in Brooklyn. Both parents were devout Catholics, and in their home in Queens they often had priests and nuns from their local church over for dinner.

After the birth of their first child, a daughter, Regina suffered two miscarriages, and the doctors told her that she would not be able to bear any more children. Regina was devastated. She had grown up close to her own younger sister—and when that sister died at sixteen, Regina vowed that if she should ever have a daughter, she would make sure that that daughter had a sister. And so when she found out she would not bear any more children, she applied to adopt a sister for her child from the New York Foundling Hospital.

Three months later she and her husband were informed that a girl was available for them.

The situation would have been perfect, except that Regina

had discovered soon after she applied for the adoption that she was pregnant again. She and Ernest almost rescinded their adoption application but decided against it, given that her pregnancy was still young and she had suffered two miscarriages already.

When they got to the Foundling Hospital, Regina was not impressed with the baby they presented her with. She thought the baby looked "rough" and "scruffy," compounded by the fact that the hospital had dressed her badly, in Regina's eyes. But Ernest liked the child right away and consoled his wife with the idea that the baby could be "cleaned up" nicely. He argued that she was the exact age that they were looking for. The nuns at the home—all white, all Sisters of the Blessed Sacrament—told the couple that the baby was named Bernadette and that the biological father of the baby was a white professor and that the biological mother was a black secretary in a school.

Regina agreed finally to accept the baby but insisted on bringing a fancy dress to the Foundling Hospital when they came to pick her up. She changed the baby's name to Carla.

The letter that Carla later obtained from the Foundling Hospital said, "Our records indicate that you were born 9/16/52, a healthy 7 lb. 5 oz. baby. You were placed in the nursery, where you were loved by the staff. Mr. and Mrs. Latty were interested in adoption, met and fell in love with you and brought you to their home. Adoption was approved."

The letter does not in any way acknowledge Regina's reservations or initially lukewarm response to the baby. It was a baby she didn't feel immediate affection for, and her original reasons for wanting the child—to provide a sibling for her daughter—were not so strong anymore, as the pregnancy seemed to be progressing. Carla Latty was the second-string baby, brought home to be a sibling to the firstborn, just in case her mother's pregnancy should not thrive.

Then not only did Regina's pregnancy thrive, resulting in another baby girl, but she and Ernest went on to have seven more children—making their brood ten in all, including Carla.

"They were part of that generation that believed they were getting as many children as God allowed," said Carla.

Though Carla's parents gave her no hint that she was not their biological child, she felt from her earliest memories that something was missing between her and her mother—there was a coldness and an unnamable distance that she could not explain. Still, she was close to her nine siblings, and of all of them, she excelled the most in both sports and academics. Her father, the police detective, was especially fond of her and took a special interest in her development. She was the only one of the children he brought with him to hear Malcolm X speak at the Audubon Ballroom in Harlem, when she was twelve. He also brought Carla and her older sister to hear Martin Luther King at the 1963 March on Washington.

Today Carla works as an attorney for a municipal workers' union in New York City. She is the only one of her siblings to have graduated from college. She went on to receive her law degree at Howard University. To this day she is the most financially solvent member of her family. Both her parents are deceased, but up until her recent death, her mother, Regina, lived with Carla and Sugar. Despite their difficult relationship, Carla had come to peace with her mother and was her primary caretaker up until her death. Given all the aid and support she'd offered to her siblings and parents over the years, I got the sense that it was Carla in fact who had adopted the family, not the other way around.

It wasn't until the age of thirty that Carla found out she was adopted.

She was temporarily living at her parents' house in Queens after just graduating from law school. One day she became terribly ill. She couldn't eat or get out of bed. Her mother was trying to give her a drink of water, and Carla wouldn't or couldn't accept it. Her mother got angry and said, "I can't deal with her," leaving the room. It was a dynamic that had played out time and time again during Carla's life—her mother becoming suddenly frustrated with Carla, as if mothering her were an enforced burden rather than a welcome role, and leaving her in the care of her father instead. Feverish, weak, perhaps more sensitive than usual because of the sickness, Carla said to her father something she had felt but had never before quite articulated: "Okay, you're my father, but she's not my mother."

It seemed on the surface just something to say, a way of returning what she felt was coldness from her mother.

But her father's response surprised her. "Who told you about that? Did your cousin tell you?"

When Carla, perplexed, asked him what he was talking about, he finally let out the truth: she was neither his biological child nor his wife's; she had been adopted as an infant. He didn't know anything about her biological parents except what the nuns at the home had told them.

Carla felt rattled, disoriented—and yet relieved, in a strange way, that what she'd sensed from her mother was not just in her mind.

What followed was a hunger that would grow in its intensity over the next twenty-odd years—a hunger to know the real story—in particular, what body she had come out of, and why her biological mother had given her away.

In 1989, when Carla was thirty-seven years old, she met the woman who would become her life companion. Crescentia Coutinho was a sparkling, vivacious Indian woman from Mumbai and of Goan descent. Carla met her at the wedding of mutual friends. They got together and stayed together and today—nineteen years later—have a rich life and deep bond. Every morning Crescentia—known as Sugar to her friends— makes Carla a cup of chai. Together they are a kind of rock— financially and emotionally—for Carla's entire brood of siblings. Sugar's family in Mumbai considers Carla one of their own, and they've traveled back and forth to India many times together.

It was Sugar who had aggressively encouraged Carla to seek out the truth of her origins. It was during their involvement that Carla began to actively pursue finding out who her birth mother and family were.

In the early eighties Carla was able to obtain a letter from the New York Foundling Hospital giving her what information they had in their records about her adoption.

"With regard to background," the letter said,

> your mother was described as a well spoken, dark skinned, 5′2″ 112 lbs. Negro woman in her late thirties. She had come to New York from the South to have her child to maintain privacy. She had been married to a White Mexican man who deserted her after the third child of their union was born. Without money or job, she placed the children, all in school, in a Catholic Institution while she went to college to become a teacher. To provide for herself and her children she taught music lessons and waitressed in order to obtain her degree. While

in college, she met a man 10 years older than she, who she said was the father of her child to be born. He was White, 5′7″, 153 lbs., had a fair complexion and was of Irish background. He expressed concern for her, however, there were no marriage plans. After your birth your mother returned to the South to teach and to provide for her three children in placement. Although she expressed sadness, she felt adoption was the best plan she could make.

In 1991, with information she obtained from an adoption rights organization, Carla was able to compare her birth certificate number with the NYC Department of Health's original birth certificate number at the New York Public Library. Only one person was born with her birth certificate number on September 16, 1952—her birthday—in New York. That person was Bernadette Senna. So she had a name, finally, but no more information than that.

More recently—when looking for further proof that this baby named Bernadette was indeed she—Carla was able to obtain her medical records from the Foundling Hospital. The records had been filled out fifty-four years before, during her first few months at the home, before she was adopted and her name had been changed. On all the pages the Foundling Hospital had blacked out her original name except for one instance, when they had inadvertently left visible her birth first name, "Bernadette Marie S." The name Bernadette was, it seems, given to her not by her birth mother, Anna, but by the director of adoptive services at the Foundling Hospital, who was also named Bernadette Marie.

Carla clung to all of this evidence of her original self, piling up the evidence when it would seem to most that she didn't need any more. When your history is erased, the scraps of information you are able to retain loom large in importance.

Over the next decade the name Senna remained an elusive clue to her identity that led nowhere.

She and Sugar embarked on a letter-writing campaign to every Senna they could find living in the United States.

They sent out a minimum of five hundred letters to Sennas all over the country. Carla would occasionally do Google searches for the name, and hits about me would inevitably come up. She read my biographical information and decided we could not be related. She was focused on looking for a sibling and saw that I had a white mother. The information about me also told her that my father was half black and half Mexican, but she didn't make the connection that my father could be one of those three older siblings mentioned in the letter, the ones with the "White Mexican" father.

They continued to search for the missing mother. Carla sensed that until she solved the mystery of where she had come from, she would not be able to move forward with her life.

Sugar meanwhile would pray during Carla's health scares that whoever Carla's mother was would watch over her.

As the search continued, Sugar kept a notebook detailing the names of all the Sennas they contacted.

My name is in that notebook, along with the date they sent the letter to me. The notation beside my name: No Reply.

Carla finally got the name of a private investigator who specialized in adoption reunions. Her name was Pamela Slaton, and according to her press release, she had solved thousands of cases. Her own interest in adoption stemmed from the fact that she had been adopted at birth and as an adult sought out her own birth family. She came up against the same barriers to finding out her biological identity as Carla had encountered: there were no records available to the children. When she did track down her biological mother, it was a terrible disappointment. Her mother was hostile and at first denied that Pamela was her daughter. Then she told her that Pamela's father was her own father as well—a sordid story that turned out to be a lie. Despite her own disastrous "reunion," Slaton decided to dedicate her life to helping other adopted children find their birth parents.

Sugar and Carla gave Slaton their information.

Slaton told them that they'd better hope that one of Carla's siblings was a boy because men didn't change their last names.

Slaton's policy was that she did not charge clients the $2,500 fee until she had success in finding their relatives.

Carla got the call on a weekday afternoon in April only a month after hiring the investigator.

"I've got good news and bad news," Slaton said to her. "Which do you want first?"

"The bad news," Carla said, bracing herself.

"The bad news? You owe me $2,500," Slaton said, without missing a beat. "The good news is I've found your family."

She gave Carla my father's e-mail address in Canada. She told Carla she had already been in touch with him and had confirmed that he and Carla had the same mother. Carla wrote to him on April 13, 2006. It also happened to be my father's sixty-second birthday.

———

My father did not show up at Baruch College until late that afternoon, many hours after he'd said he would be there. He called my cell phone to say he was parked downstairs. Sugar, Carla, and I went down on the elevator to meet him.

I saw him through the glass doors, and he was wearing a three-piece suit. Sometimes, from a distance, I was able to see it—how he might appear to a stranger. His features were striking—a mixture of many continents.

Carla, tiny, bespectacled, serious, let out a slight gasp at the sight of my father. He was—after me—the first biological family member she'd ever laid eyes on. He was her long-lost brother whom she had never met. My father still seemed skeptical, however, and stiffly shook their hands and avoided eye contact.

Back in the conference room he sat down and began talking. He talked without pause for an hour. I was embarrassed by his lateness, anxious that he was talking so much, but when I looked around I saw that Carla and Sugar were listening, rapt. They were of course fascinated by what he had to tell them about the family history. But perhaps what struck me most, as I sat there listening to my father talk, was that this was the first time I could recall being in the company of adults for whom my father was blood. Carla was his sister, and although it had taken her half a century to meet him, she was a part of my father and he was a part of her.

That afternoon, in the fading light of the Baruch College conference room, he told us rambling, circular tales about his childhood. He didn't pause to ask Carla how she had found him or what her life had been up until this moment. Little bits of intriguing information flew into the air like sparks off a railroad track. His mother, he said, smoked Lucky Strikes and Pall Malls, unfiltered. After they moved up north, she was the only black person working in the traffic clerk's office in Boston. It was a hostile white Irish atmosphere. She had gotten the job the same way she had gotten every other lucky break in her life, it seemed—through Father Ryan. She rose up from a lowly clerk to a supervisor. She had been a musical prodigy in her youth and could play opera, classical, and jazz on the piano, as well as the violin, the flute, and the trombone. She could hear a song once and play it through to the end. She had a retiring personality and hated any sort of conflict. She died slowly, agonizingly, in August 1972 in our family's big old house on Robeson Street in Jamaica Plain, a working-class neighborhood in Boston. She grew increasingly ill when the oxygen tanks they'd been delivering to the house became no longer effective. The painkillers no longer worked. Finally he brought her to St. Joseph's Hospital in Brighton, where she died. She had asked that her remains be cremated and deposited off the coast of Marblehead.

My father said that he did not remember his father, Francisco, but had been told that they'd lived in New York for several years. He remembered Hispanic people, Spanish voices, but remembered only two incidents clearly from that time. One was in a cafeteria, when he was supposed to have been watching his baby sister, and she fell off a table and hit her head and had to go to the hospital. He got in trouble.

"I goofed," he told Carla, Sugar, and me. And the phrase *I goofed* made it seem that he was in a strange trance of memory. It was the language of a young boy, the words he'd likely used to explain it to his mother at the time. "Ma got really upset. I never forgot it."

The other incident he remembered from his childhood was in a train station. His mother had gone to a desk to get directions, and my father and his sibling got lost in a crowd. A Hispanic woman grabbed them both and began to walk off with them. His mother ran after them. "Those are my children," Anna yelled. The Hispanic woman said, "These aren't yours. They don't look like you." A policeman approached and leaned down and said, "Okay, guys, which one is your mother?" And my father and his sibling ran to Anna. "I only remember it was cold and I didn't like it."

My father had been talking for about an hour at this point. While he took a sip of water, I interrupted. "Papa, you should see the letter Carla brought from the orphanage about her origins."

Carla pulled out the letter and handed my father a copy.

He put on his reading glasses and read in silence, his mouth turned down in concentration. When he was finished, his whole affect had changed. Some hard wall fell away. His face was fighting against emotion. He looked bewildered and excited and sad. "Will you look at that," he said, looking between the letter and Carla's face. "You're my sister."

And he stood up and hugged Carla for the first time since his arrival.

Carla was the missing link we'd all been waiting for. She was the warm body of evidence that we needed to fill in the gaps in Anna's story. But questions swirled around us all as we parted ways on the New York City street, promising to stay in touch.

The biggest question for my father was whether he was a full sibling to Carla—and therefore also the son of Father Ryan—or whether he was just a half sibling. And what about his other siblings? How related were they all to one another? Had Anna been telling the truth about a Mexican boxer? Had he even existed?

Had she had three children by Francisco José, and was Carla just the accident with the priest at the end?

Months later, my father, Carla, and his other sibling each got swabbed for a DNA test to find out the answer to how related they were. The test results showed that my father's younger sibling and Carla share both parents.

My father is a half sibling to them.

This means my father is most likely the only child of Francisco José Senna and Anna.

The others (one of them, the third child, the daughter before Carla, refused to be tested at all) were most likely the product of Anna's relationship with the priest, Father Ryan. He was, we could assume, the white man described in that orphanage letter—"5'7", 153 lbs. . . . [of] fair complexion and . . . of Irish background," the one who "expressed concern" for Anna, but with whom "there were no marriage plans."

But of course Father Ryan was dead, his body of evidence long gone cold, and so, it seemed, he was protected in death by the lie he'd told while he'd been alive.

I gave birth in August to a healthy eight-pound-three-ounce baby boy. He came two weeks early—which was, according to the doctor, lucky for me, given his size.

They say it takes time to love your baby. But my husband and I immediately fell in love with him. I kept bursting into tears that first week as I nursed him. The thought that kept going through my head: *I chose to bring you here.* My husband and I lay in bed staring at him each morning, marveling at the power of bringing a human being into the world.

Over the weeks and months that followed, I noticed people—strangers, friends—commenting on his appearance, the way they always do with babies, but I heard hints, imagined or not, of the old racial curiosity.

A white woman on the street glanced into his stroller, smiling, but did a double take at the sight of him. She looked between my face and his and said, "Is his daddy black?" I hesitated, thrown off by her question, then said, "Yes, so is his mother." The woman looked confused but I didn't elaborate.

Others, people I knew, seemed surprised by his pale ("fair") complexion and his light-colored hair.

"He's so pale."

"Is his hair going to stay that color?"

A friendly acquaintance called me during my first week home from the hospital to congratulate me on the baby. She wanted to know what the baby looked like. She asked several times what his hair looked like. She wanted to know why I had not posted pictures with the e-mailed birth announcement. I could not say why, only that something had made me hesitate. Some instinct made me want to protect him from the curious eyes of the world as long as I could. All around the world, in so many different cultures, there is a belief in the evil eye—and women in Russia traditionally waited forty days to show the baby to anyone outside the immediate circle. My desire to keep the baby hidden was perhaps a bit of that ancient impulse, but something else too, something more specific to do with race and color that I could not articulate.

The next day another friend—someone mixed, like me—proclaimed, upon seeing the baby naked, in particular seeing his scrotum, which was darker than the rest of his body, that this was proof that he would darken up.

I covered the baby's body with a blanket, feeling a rush of protective rage, as if the observation itself were a violation.

But there was nothing I could do, because it had already begun, the attaching of racial meaning to his features when the child had barely just lost his umbilical cord.

People were interested in what side of the road his racial features would fall. Would he darken up? Would his baby hair fall out and an Afro grow in its place?

I found myself surprised by how alienated I felt from these questions. After a lifetime of being similarly obsessed by race and color, a lifetime of being the one asking these very questions of others, I found myself hostile to the interest when it came to my own child. It's not that I wasn't curious about what he would look like. But suddenly the racial interest—even from the most benign sources—felt like a kind of corruption to me.

Never has the perversity of racialized thinking been so clear as when it is being applied to a newborn baby.

But I also know it's possible I'm paranoid. I also know it's possible I am imagining things.

A friend came over to meet the baby. She is beautiful, black, with rich brown skin the color of my grandmother's. I bring her into the living room and stand back so she can see my baby. She is quiet for a beat, and I think I see a flicker of something—disappointment? surprise?—cross her face. I imagine she wishes my baby had come out browner, blacker-featured, whatever that means. No, that can't be true. She says he's adorable, and yet there's a quizzical expression on her face when she says it. A few weeks later she calls to see if she can come visit. She asks me if the baby has changed.

What do you mean by "changed"? I ask.

"Have his lips gotten any fuller?" she wants to know. "Has his skin darkened up?"

So no, it is not in my mind. I am picking up something undeniable in her tone. People see my baby, and in the face of his racial ambiguity their own past hurts, desires, fears, and fantasies rise to the surface. He—the baby—becomes the Rorschach inkblot upon which all of their own projections come to the surface.

But I know it isn't just them. It's also me.

My father's racial obsessions live in me.

He passed them down to me just the way he passed down his eczema and asthma. In lieu of an inheritance, I have his diseases as proof that I am his daughter.

I live three thousand miles away from the scene of the crime. My baby is a California creation. His middle name is Lakota—the Sioux word for "friend."

I don't care about the color of his skin or the texture of his hair. I want him to be kind. I want him to laugh a lot. I want him to be lucky, and I want him to be resilient. I want him to love deeply and be loved.

The other morning the baby smiled at us for the first time in a way that seemed not just like gas but like he was really responding to the funny faces we were making at him. I wondered aloud why that smile of his was so heartbreakingly sweet. My husband said it was because there was no history behind it. "It's a smile with no history," he said. And, he added, without history there is no irony. It was a smile with no irony.

One morning I wistfully mentioned to my husband that I wanted our son to know the weather of the East Coast, the snow and the rain that I grew up around. My husband shook his head and said, "I want a California kid. I want snow to be something he's heard of." And after he said it, I knew that I wanted a California kid too. I wouldn't be here if I didn't want that. Snow. Yes, something he has heard of. And snow seemed to me in that moment, standing on a Venice street loading the cheery red stroller into the back of the car, to be code for something else, history maybe. I want history to be something he's heard of, read about, knowledgeable about, but something he's not confined by, controlled by, limited by. And of course I know this is impossible.

I am protective of his freedom to define himself in a way I

never could do myself. I am angered by the judgments, expectations, and assumptions made about him in a way I have never felt angered on my own behalf.

I am aware, each time it happens, that my parents not only did not take offense at the projections thrown onto me, my sister, and my brother—they instigated them, courted them. They supplied us with a language for what we were before we could talk, so we had no hope of defining ourselves outside such definitions, no hope of feeling free of such a world of labels. We were there for the world's taking.

My husband has rented a Volvo for our Christmas holiday in Martha's Vineyard. He rented a Volvo to please me, and I think, as I sit on its heated leather seat beside him, that it's the kindest thing anybody has ever done for me. He remembered something I said to him a long time ago, a fantasy I described to him before I even got pregnant—a silly fantasy I had of us driving up to my mother's house in a Volvo station wagon with a baby in our backseat. In my fantasy it was summer, and it is winter here now—the island is emptied out, barren, like a photographic negative of itself—but it doesn't matter, because I am in a silver Volvo with my husband beside me and our baby is cooing in the backseat and I feel like I'm in the car commercial of my dreams as we wind along the country road toward my mother's house. My brother and my sister and their children are all there. We will have a rare reunion with the newest generation of cousins together for the first time. I can almost hear the soundtrack that accompanies us as we drive along State Road, can almost hear the voice-over describing the car's virtues.

I've been susceptible to car commercial fantasies ever since I was small. Car commercials and sitcoms and movie families have embedded themselves under my skin. I used to whine and plead with my eccentric mother, "Why can't you be a real mother?" Real to me was what I saw on TV. And right now, from where I sit in this Volvo, it feels like maybe I've made it, I'm finally there, living inside the car commercial, not on the outside anymore.

Volvos have a particularly special place in my imagination. They were the cars driven by the fathers I never had—fathers with sensible shoes and kind eyes who loved their daughters, preparing them for a life of loving men who loved them back. As we drive toward our destination, it does cross my mind that my husband looks not like those white dads of my youth but rather like my own father, the same copper skin tone, the same soft black curls, the same vaguely mixed features. And so perhaps I've rewritten history by making a black man who looks like my father drive a Volvo.

It's raining when we arrive at my mother's house on the West Tisbury–Chilmark border. It's a classic Cape Cod house, the kind with weathered brown shingles and white window boxes. Tonight the windows glow yellow. I can just make out the edge of a lit Christmas tree inside. It looks like a gingerbread cottage under the rain-darkened sky. It looks like a house from a dream or a fairy tale, like a place where nothing bad can happen.

But as we pull into the driveway, something interrupts my reverie: my three-year-old nephew comes running around the side of the house with his hair soaking wet, naked from the waist down, in a T-shirt and a pair of mud-drenched socks. He's laughing and screaming, and my mother is on his heels. She looks wild herself, with a blue bruise on her chin and her blond hair wild and tangled around her face. Through the windshield

I watch as she grabs him and tries to drag him back inside the house. The child flails and tries to break free, his face alight with taunting laughter.

For a moment I had forgotten how mad my family is—all of them—how far from a car commercial we really are.

The Volvo's engine is still running, and we watch my nephew break loose from my mother's arms and run off screaming naked through the rain, and my mother seems to finally see us parked there in front of her. She wipes wet hair out of her face and gives us a weary smile.

"You can turn off the engine now," I say to my husband, who is still sitting inside the car, his hand frozen on the key, staring out at the rain.

We have our Christmas Eve dinner in the clutter of my mother's house. She and my brother have pushed a series of small tables together so that it has the feeling of a long line of child's tables rather than one adult one. My cousin Rebecca and her husband Jeff and their daughter Iris have come from New York City. They are white and Jewish and add to the feeling that none of the parts fit together.

My sister's three children are half Pakistani, and they all live in England. My brother is married to a woman who is half Chinese and half white, and they have a nine-month-old daughter named Xing. My father is there too. He showed up at the crack of dawn this morning, without warning, after a thirty-six-hour bus trip from Canada, wearing a rumpled suit. My sister glanced out the window to see him meandering across the lawn, like the ghost of Christmas past, like Lov Bensey of *Tobacco Road*, who walks seven miles home eating a raw winter turnip.

Tomorrow, his long-lost sister, Carla, the secret child of his black mother and the Irish priest, will show up on the island with her Indian girlfriend. They too are part of this picture now.

That night my father and my mother sit at one table like husband and wife, surrounded by their children and grandchildren. All of the children are sick with the flu, and they take turns sticking their germy fingers in the baby Xing's mouth. My father cuts the chicken and serves tiny portions to the hungry guests. There really isn't enough food for this many people, and so we each eat a dollhouse version of a meal: on each plate a few peas, a teaspoon of mashed potatoes, a single cut of chicken, a paper-thin slice of beet. Nobody has dared to mention that there isn't enough food except one of the children, who screams, "I'm still hungry!" while the rest of us smile and nod and cut the tiny bits of food into even tinier pieces, trying to make it last the length of a normal meal.

A few years ago, in this same house, a white man tried to break in during the night. I awoke to my mongrel dog barking and the sound of somebody trying to remove the screen from the window. He was an island drifter who had developed an obsession with me based on our small interactions at the corner store, where our dogs would play together. Now, seated here, I imagine somebody, maybe that intruder, staring in at us all. I wonder what the person on the outside would make of this motley group—if they would see a table of strangers, or if they would know, from the way we interact, from the invisible history that echoes through our every interaction, that we are family, that we have known each other for a long, long time, that we have always been linked.

Some of us are linked by blood and are only now just meeting. Others are linked through the pain as much as the joy we've brought one another. There is *history* at this table. My mother has a bruise on her chin from the three-year-old's head butt. It is a fresh mark, but I can't look at it without remembering the ancient, now faded bruises my father inflicted on her face and body once upon a time with his fist. There are reverberations here in this room. My sister and I barely speak. We have hurt each other too. My brother and his wife hide in the bedroom, enraged at my mother and sister for letting the other children infect Xing, their baby. My infant son stares around the table with the biggest, blackest eyes I've ever seen on a child, his plump lower lip falling out, adding to the aura of bewilderment on his face. My cousin's daughter—the Jewish one with the bright red hair—is only eleven but has recently declared herself a lesbian. She is dressed in drag today, the way she dresses every day, hoping to confuse strangers into calling her "sir," as the waiter did at her eleventh birthday dinner, to which she wore a suit. Her father jokes around and says she is the son he never had. She is a child out of a Woody Allen movie, all sardonic and alienated and wisecracking. She has written a novel and wants me to blurb it. My sister's children, the Pakistani-English cousins, seem quaint, old-fashioned in comparison, like characters from one of the *Noddy* books we used to read as children.

In this spirit, perhaps, the English-Pakistani cousins have brought from across the ocean a Golliwog doll—coal-black face, white bug eyes, red felt smile, a snappy pinstriped suit. They present it to their cousin Xing as a gift. My brother loves it and says, "Anybody who finds him offensive can get the fuck out!" My sister informs us all that the term *wog* is not so offensive as it seems. She says the letters stand for Westernized Oriental Gentleman. Somebody has propped the Wog on top of the

Christmas tree in lieu of a northern star. I look at the racist car-icature strung up in the tree and think it's a kind of inverse of Billie Holiday's "Strange Fruit." The multiracial family has lynched a Golliwog tonight, put him in his place. My sister's three children, three Westernized Oriental gentle boys and girl, sit together beneath this tree shaking presents and trying to guess the contents. A palpable excitement is building among the Jewish and Muslim brethren of our clan on this most Christian of holidays. As dessert is served—the only part of the meal dur-ing which we actually have enough for everybody—the three-year-old runs across the room and does a flying leap into the pile of presents. We all wince at the sound of breaking valuables, crunching boxes, ripping wrapping paper, destroyed gifts. My mother rushes toward the child, where he lies on the heap, flailing his legs and laughing maniacally, and drags him into another room for a time-out. My sister, disapproving but not rising from her seat, sighs and rolls her eyes and says to nobody in particular: "My mother just loves to discipline my children."

Despite these craggy moments, or perhaps because of them, I have the sense as we sit together that maybe this dinner is a victory—a sign that we have survived the terrible blows we have inflicted upon one another, that we have wrestled history itself, in all of its brutality and all its deceptions, to the ground. I imagine there is a sign above the table reading, "Anybody who finds this offensive can get the fuck out." Tonight this awkward, meager meal is a victory so subtle, you might just miss it if you weren't looking.

The next day, however, the war is back on.

My mother calls my hotel room at the crack of dawn cursing

into the phone against my father, who has somehow convinced her to loan him her car.

"I'm freezing my ass off at the ferry. He was supposed to be here an hour ago."

She's talking too fast for me to understand exactly what has happened. Something about my father wanting to leave the island with his newfound sister, Carla, and her girlfriend for the day, but needing to borrow my mother's car so that he can get the residential cheap rate on the ferry ticket. Only it was a trick, she says—a trick to get her to actually pay the ferry fee on her credit card. And now they are an hour late, and she is waiting in the cold for them to come get the car and take it off the island so that they can go meet with some relative of Father Ryan's who has offered to help them prove once and for all the dead priest is her father.

I get off the phone with her and realize I'm strangely relieved to have things back to normal, strangely relieved to hear my mother spitting out invectives against my father, just like old times, relieved to have my father in grifter mode again, still trying to hoodwink her out of the imaginary Wasp inheritance he believes she possesses.

I get dressed, and my husband and I and the baby head down to meet her at the ferry, where we find her still waiting, pacing in the cold, cursing under her fog of white breath.

"I don't have all day. Where the hell are they?" She glances at her watch.

"Why did you agree to this?"

"Because it costs less if you're a resident, and—" She stops, hears herself. "I don't know. I'm a fool."

Just then my father appears. He's crossing the street, all dressed up like a foreign dignitary in a long black wool coat, a dark business suit, his hair shining and coiffed, his skin waxy with face cream. He doesn't seem to notice us and walks past us, toward the row of cars waiting to get on the ferry.

My mother calls out his name.

He turns and, with a nod, spins on his heel, and starts toward us to get the car key from my mother.

Trailing him at a distance are his newfound sisters. They are all gussied up—makeup, silk scarves, long flowing coats. Sugar, Carla's girlfriend, seems titillated by the prospect of an adventure. Carla looks more dubious.

Sugar kisses us, leaving marks of lipstick on our cheeks and perfume in the air around us. Breathless, she says, "When big brother calls, we must follow!" before rushing to catch up with my father.

After discovering his lost half sister, my father became obsessed with trying to prove the biological link between Carla and Father Ryan. Though it seemed obvious that the letter Carla received from the Foundling Home was referring to Father Ryan, he remains unnamed, their relationship left out of the history in the form of these frayed and few documents. There seemed to be no physical proof that he had fathered Anna's children. My father—who had grown up in the culture where powerful white men routinely preyed sexually on black women, impregnated them, then denied the existence of their mixed-race children—was on a mission to see the truth about Father Ryan and Anna brought into the cold, harsh light of day.

In lieu of a DNA test, my father brought the story to the media. He pitched an article about Carla and her discovery to *The Boston Globe*. The journalist he corresponded with followed up and published a large Lifestyle piece in November of 2006 called "Mother and Father." The subhead read: "At 30, Carla Latty learned she was adopted. Now she's trying to unravel a bigger secret."

Ed Devine, eighty-six years old, lives in Foxboro, Massachusetts. He is Father Ryan's first cousin and one of the last of their generation in the Ryan family. His mother was a sister of Francis Ryan's father. When he happened to read *The Boston Globe* article about Carla, he contacted the paper and asked the reporter for permission to get in touch with my father. He wanted to help Carla in whatever way he could.

When my father and Carla and Sugar left the island that day in my mother's car, they were headed to Foxboro to meet Mr. Devine at his home. They already knew he would be of no use in establishing the DNA connection. In order to prove her biological connection to Father Ryan, Carla needed to have the DNA of a relative who was descended through the male line. Still, Devine was the first relative she would meet from the Ryan side of her bloodline.

Carla and Sugar later recounted to me what happened that day off the island. The three of them piled into my mother's Toyota RAV, my father at the wheel. They found their way to Ed Devine's house, where the feisty old man explained why he'd contacted the *Globe*. He said he was sympathetic to Carla's search for the truth because he and his wife had taken in foster children over the years, and he understood what it was to be separated from one's family. He was warm, open, and friendly, seeming to enjoy their company and attention as he rattled on about his relationship to Father Ryan. At some point he mentioned that there was, in fact, another first cousin of Father Ryan's still living—in Foxboro, as a matter of fact: Charles

"Charlie" Ryan, whose father was the brother of Father Ryan's father. My father and Carla and Sugar gave one another excited looks: this was the direct male-line descendant they had hoped to find. My father asked Devine to call Charlie Ryan and see if they could visit him. The old man shrugged and said he didn't even have Charles Ryan's phone number anymore. My father picked up the phone and called information and got the number, shoved the receiver at the old man, and told him he could call his cousin now.

The old man dialed. "Charlie," he said into the receiver. "You still alive?"

Ed Devine didn't get a chance to explain to Charlie the full story before my father and Carla and Sugar were out the door, on their way. They sped to the address of Charlie Ryan. They found him there, a decrepit old man in an armchair who seemed confused by the huddle of brown faces in his living room. They showed him the *Globe* article, which my father had in his briefcase. Charlie was able only to glance at it with this group of strangers hovering, impatient, around him.

"What can I do to help you?" he asked.

My father was already pulling the Q-tips out of his bag.

He told Charlie he needed his DNA to prove the link between Carla and Father Ryan. He told Charlie to open wide. He gave Charlie a cotton swab, and the old man dutifully scraped the insides of his cheeks, while my father hovered at his side.

Carla whispered to my father that this DNA sample might not stand up in a court of law.

My father shushed her, told her he knew what he was doing. "This is what they use on crime scenes."

Carla didn't protest.

After Charlie handed over his saliva-coated cotton swab, my

father asked him to get him some Saran Wrap from the kitchen. Charlie, still looking bewildered, obediently rose and hobbled to the kitchen, returning a few minutes later with the box of cling wrap. My father used it to wrap up the sample—which, my father hoped, would be the physical evidence that Father Ryan was Carla's real father.

My father was able to get the head of Father Ryan's Josephite order to cover the $500 DNA test. In the end, it successfully established the link proving that at least two of Anna's children were related to Father Ryan by blood.

We learn in school that the civil rights movement was about overcoming segregation. But as my father has pointed out to me, what an oddly neutral word—*segregation*—to describe what was happening in this country. We prefer it to more blunt descriptions of that social arrangement: subjugation, oppression. And perhaps, also, we don't want to acknowledge the ways in which we were not segregated at all, the ways in which the lives of black and white people have always been intertwined at the most intimate level. Slavery was intimate. Oppression is so often an act of intimacy.

Later I learned that Father Ryan's term as priest at St. John the Baptist in Montgomery was from 1930 to 1939, a particularly fraught time in Alabama's racial history. It was during those same years that Montgomery and the nation saw the famous Scottsboro Trial, when nine black youths were sentenced to death for the alleged rape of two white women. While white men of some power like Father Ryan were regularly and secretly engaging in sexual relationships with black women, the preoccupation of the day was with black men preying on white women.

In his book *Desegregating the Altar: The Josephites and the Struggle for Black Priests, 1871–1960,* published in 1990, Stephen Ochs talks about race and the Josephite mission to integrate the Catholic Church. He is candid about the racism of the church—the Josephites were happy to convert blacks, but they resisted for a long time allowing black men to become priests. Part of their reasoning: a racist fear that black men would be unable to maintain their celibacy.

One day I called Stephen Ochs, chair of the history department at Georgetown Preparatory School, to ask him if, in his research, he had come upon evidence of sexual relationships between white priests and black women during the Josephite "colored harvest" missions. He seemed affronted by the question and said he had never heard of any such impropriety.

Father Ryan's obituary, of course, says nothing about his relationship with my grandmother. Rather, it lauds him as a paterfamilias of the black community. In a newsletter put out by the Josephites called, eerily, *Colored Harvest,* Father Ryan's life in the rural South is described: "He is rich in health, has his horse and dog, and goes about in perfect contentment, smoking his pipe, unhurried, a picture of frugality and patience, a friend to all."

All my life I have listened to my father blame his every misdeed and failing on society—racism, poverty—never on himself. His problems were largely social and political issues. The fact that he'd been abusive to my mother, and that he'd been unable to support his family—these were, according to him, problems of society. When I wrote him letters trying to force him to confront his behavior, he would send me back a treatise on racism and poverty and social forces.

And in a sense, as I stare at the pictures of him in the orphanage, as I travel down south where I can smell the ghost of strange fruit, can taste the oppression on my tongue, I know there is a certain truth to his perspective, even as it leaves me unsatisfied, even as it leaves me unable to move on. He may have his reasons, but knowing this has not healed us. Redemption eludes us. What is the opposite of redemption? Stasis? I'm not sure. I only know that we are stuck.

I feel at times like Dorothy in *The Wizard of Oz* looking behind the curtain. I see the old man pulling the levers of my emotions, pumping out smoke of politics and racial theories, flashing mirrors on me with distorted images. He is revealed to me. But what do I do now that I have seen the man behind the curtain?

My father, as far as I can tell, has expressed to me no guilt or remorse for what he did to our family. Is there such a thing as punishment without guilt? I spent a lifetime hardening myself to the man, hating him as a form of self-preservation—because to love him would mean to hate my mother, who was my life-line to sanity, the outside world—and if I learned one thing from my parents, it was that you could not love both of them. My siblings and I were simply not allowed to do it. And so we split ourselves, our lives. We cleaved ourselves. *Cleave*: to split, to make something split, especially along a plane of natural weakness. In the cleaving, my sister chose my father, and how could she not? Same designation in a crowd of screaming red Irish faces, or a room of tight-lipped dismissive Wasps who assume their own significance and wit and intelligence as if they were still central, despite the evidence to the contrary.

I, on the other hand, worked hard to hate him. It *was* hard work, because he transgressed so many times against my mother's impression of him. In those moments he offered gestures of love that made the hating more difficult. And there was the deep intelligence too—the incisive commentary on the world that formed my own, whether I liked it or not. Because I am his black creation at the end of the day: without him I would be nothing—a Wasp with a permanent tan; without him I would have no point of view, no fire. That gift from him was offered without generosity, just sent down as unintentionally as big flat feet or high cheekbones. No, that's not true. Perhaps it was intentional, the only gift he knew how to give—his fire this time, and the flat feet, and a desk that might never come together. But at least, when years later I did finally sit down to write, it guaranteed that I would have something to say and the urgency to say it.

I didn't get the birthday gifts from him I wanted, ever; I never got the desk I wanted, preassembled, white-glove delivery service. But he gave me gifts I cannot deny. It wasn't just knowledge or fire he passed down, it was also pedestrian, poverty-stricken attempts at love: a trip to a trendy clothing store; cash handed over one afternoon, drunkenly, to go furnish his apartment so that it would be someplace I wasn't ashamed to bring my friends to. I grabbed the cash, but my sister stopped me, she alone knowing that we mustn't spend this money, we mustn't take advantage of a man when he was inebriated and desperate to please us. He wanted us to be proud of that apartment. Wanted two children, ten and eleven, to go to a furniture store with hundreds of dollars in cash and buy whatever we wanted. Those gestures thwarted my hatred, but it always came back; I found a way to see that nothing he offered would ever be enough. My mother's terror; her permanently crooked nose, broken by his fist; her rage—I took it on as my own so that nothing he did or purchased would ever be enough to make up for that debt.

Sometimes he would look at me and name it. "You hate me, don't you? Nothing I do will ever be enough." And I would scoff and say that wasn't true, but we both knew it was. Didn't he understand I was trying to save my own life? Spare myself from the anger. Spare myself from the violence and the loneliness and the disappointment of loving him. I never knew back then that he'd spent a portion of his childhood in an orphanage, but I sensed that to ally myself with him would be to orphan myself.

Anna, Carla, my father—they had all been orphaned in

some way. And my father had always had an orphan's perspective on the world. To love him would be to become him, another Dickensian child fogging up the glass of the restaurant window with hot hungry breath. I accepted his gifts, the fury and the fire, but I wanted a proper desk to write it on, and because he failed to give me this, I could not thank him for the rest.

Today, my father and I have a distant, cautious relationship, not unlike that of many women I know with their own fathers, especially when divorce is in their history. My father and I are cordial most of the time. He sends me news clippings via e-mail. Sometimes they are about our old obsession of race; more often than not, they are fatherly in their concerns; such as a report on the most unhealthy cities to live in the nation or an article about cancer-causing plastics.

He is preoccupied with questions of his own health and aging. He lives a quiet life with his second wife in the Canadian Maritimes. They share a suburban home with a floral sofa surrounded by wifely bric-a-brac, a porcelain doll in a hoop dress, embroidered pillows. There he sits watching news reports on the country he left behind.

Since he left the United States, I have been up to Canada to visit him only once. I had to take two flights to get to the closest airport, which was still several hours' drive from his small town. When I got off the airplane, I saw him standing beside the baggage carousel talking to a young black man with dreadlocks. He was shaking the man's hand. Later, in the car, as we drove along a winding road marked by MOOSE X-ING signs, he told me the man was one of the only other black people in this area. They'd seen each other before a few times and spoken. They were as different as two men could be. The man was thirty years younger than my father, an immigrant from the West Indies who drove a taxicab for a living—but in the Canadian Maritimes, he and my father couldn't help but acknowledge each other, fellow dark strangers in a strange land.

It was winter. The sky was a slate nothingness, the trees were mostly bare, there was frost on the windshield. He wore a look of sadness and regret that seemed new to me, though perhaps I had simply never noticed before. And although he talked with great enthusiasm about his new home, his new life in this foreign but not-so-foreign nation, I sensed homesickness beneath his demeanor.

He kept asking me what people in the United States "were saying" about this hot political issue or that, as if there were a collective opinion on the streets or as if there were people huddled together on street corners across the United States sharing their opinions with one another. As we drove, he made jokes about race, politics, and history, the way he always has with me, but there was a hunger in the jokes, as if he had not had the company of anybody in a long time who got them.

In the Canadian Maritimes, he is not just the only black man at the dinner party. He is the only black man in the world. His wife, blond, slender, kind, and comforting, springs from a history unrelated to the one he has fled. He lives with strangers, removed from any familiar context. It is as if he has joined the witness protection program. He has finally cut himself off from the center of the storm, cast himself loose from the problem. He has finally escaped America—but did he choose to leave it, or did it chase him away?

And yet the world he has landed in is not entirely strange. His new wife comes from a large Catholic family. Though she is white and a product of Canada, she represents in many ways the same class and culture that he was raised in down South. My mother was more the foreigner. I sense that this new wife understands him better, that they are more in sync in terms of the daily domestic rituals that make a marriage.

I stayed up there only a few days. He complained the whole time that he wished I could be there longer. He seemed excited to show me off to his wife's family, and to show off to me the world he had made there with her. He explained to me what they ate together in the evenings. He showed me the review he'd just published in *The Globe and Mail* about a new book on Islam and jihad. He seemed hungry for intellectual discussion. He told me he thought religion served one good function, and that was to comfort people in old age. He said it was good for the elderly. He said he thought marriages worked only when each person had a clearly defined role. He said the problem that his and my mother's generation had made was to think marriage could be equal.

The day before I left, he brought me to the gym where he and his wife go several times a week to exercise. There I sat side by side with his wife on exercise bikes, and we watched my father in the pool through the glass wall next to us as he swam his laps. She chatted to me about her efforts to keep him healthy. She told me she'd gotten him to eat oatmeal every morning for breakfast. She said: "Your father talks about you all the time. He tells everyone we meet about you and your accomplishments. He's so proud of you. You should hear him go on."

I watched him through the glass, his arms rising and falling, slicing through the water, and felt my own smallness. I wondered if I would ever be able to rise above the past, to let go of my rage against him, my mother's rage against him, long enough to feel proud of all that he had pulled off: his sobriety, a real marriage in a new land with a good woman, his ability to keep reinventing himself, even now.

The bedsheets in the guestroom where I slept that night smelled so familiar, smelled of him, of the old apartment I used to stay at on Cypress Street, and as sad as that space is in my memory, the smell of the sheets reminded me that that old apartment had, in spite of everything, been a home to me.

On my last day, we left the house for the airport when it was still dark. My father seemed sad, drove with his head cocked to the side, his mouth turned down in melancholy. I wanted coffee. He brought me to a nearby Tim Hortons coffee shop and ordered donuts and coffee for both of us, but when the cashier rang us up, my father expected me to pay for us both. The cup of coffee, the donuts, a sum of money so trivial—and yet I felt it, the old snapping anger in my brain, the rage that can go into remission but is never really gone. I still wanted him to pay me back for the childhood that was long since over.

In the spring of 1972 my father returned briefly to the south. He went to teach for the summer in New Orleans, one of the few temporary locales he remembers with fondness from his childhood. Back then my father had lived in Houma with the woman he called Ma Verrett, that beautiful aging mistress to the white senator. But times had changed, and the social revolution was in full swing. My father rented a room in a hippie commune in New Orleans and taught a summer creative writing course at Xavier University, the black Catholic college his mother had attended while he and his siblings were in the Zimmer Home.

Up north at his home in Boston that summer, my mother was pregnant with my brother, her third child, and taking care of Anna, who was slowly succumbing to complications from her cancers and surgeries. My father's class at Xavier was the university's first creative writing course, and at the end of it, with a grant from the National Endowment for the Arts, he published a literary journal of his students' work called *Parachute Shop Blues*. He dedicated the journal to his mother, Anna M. Senna, class of 1954.

On the last page of the journal, he published one of his own poems called "The Corner of Goodbye," which seems to me now a kind of requiem for the marriage that was already crumbling, or maybe for the beloved and enigmatic mother who he knew wasn't going to live much longer.

> Can you get over the despairing view of
> affection?
> Can you get over,
> in the violent lakes of June,
> Venus alone in the dusk?
> Since the sleep that turns to sadness
> returns to sleep, we
> Must anticipate ourselves as the point
> Of a seasonal joke.
>
> My hand will stretch outside my dream
> Into a cool white muslim crater.
> There is no way to compute the next
> world that we'll find,
> or live without changing feelings.

After his class at Xavier ended, he rushed home to find Anna sicker than ever, hooked up to an oxygen tank in her bedroom on the second floor of our house. She died that August. A few months later my brother was born into their already-crumbling marriage. Our parents named him Maceo, inspired both by James Brown's horn player, Maceo Parker, and by the Afro-Cuban revolutionary Antonio Maceo.

In the months before his mother's death, my father had gone on a pilgrimage to try to find out more about his elusive past. He drove in his red Mustang convertible, first to Washington,

D.C., to the Mexican Embassy, where a man who worked there called Señor Madrid recalled meeting his father and his mother when they were together. He showed my father news clippings about Francisco José, and he saw in photographs that they had the same two-toned upper lip, light on one side, dark on the other. After D.C. he went south to Louisiana and Alabama, where he gathered documents of his childhood and photographs of Anna as a young girl. In the mid-seventies, he went on his second pilgrimage. He was grieving this time too, but it was my mother who was gone. In the aftermath of one of his violent drinking binges, she had fled town with us kids and settled in Connecticut, where her sister lived. This time my father drove all the way down to Monterrey, Mexico, in search of his Mexican ancestors but had no luck.

My father kept a file of notes and documents from this research, but in the hard years that followed—as he struggled with divorce, poverty, alcoholism—he moved from apartment to flophouse to couch and put his things in storage. He couldn't hold a job. He couldn't stay sober. He moved so much, the storage company lost track of where to send his bills and his payments lapsed. When he finally returned to reclaim his boxes, which held those few shreds of evidence he'd gathered of his story, the storage company had thrown them away.

When he began to recover and get his life together in 1983, he wrote to the Mexican Embassy, asking for the news clippings that Señor Madrid had shown him. The reply was disheartening.

As Sr. Madrid which you mention in your letter passed away in 1976, we consulted our file and found a reference card on Francisco SENNA (a) "Cisco Kid" and, in Sr. Madrid's handwriting, "Fcc. (short name for Francisco) GUERRERO Senna." The above reference card only mentions that sometime in 1944 this Francisco SENNA (a) "Cisco Kid" requested protection to our Consulate General in Los Angeles, Cal. We found no newspaper clippings of any kind. We came to the conclusion that this person have [*sic*] to be your father, as the alias "Cisco Kid" would be one a professional fighter would use.

The only person besides his mother ever to admit having met his elusive Mexican father had died, and all that was left, once again, were teasing, insubstantial allusions to his existence.

My father never gave up trying to find out more about his paternity. New tidbits of information emerged, linking him to this elusive grifter father. Through computer research, he found a small faded document online. It was a scan of an old government card, dated November 19, 1952, a RECORD OF ALIEN ADMITTED FOR TEMPORARY STAY presented in Laredo, Texas. The name on it is Francisco Señina-Guerrero, aka Senna, Joaquin, aka Kid Senna. It was an application for my grandfather to "live and work" in the United States. It was one of millions of applications filled out by Mexicans hoping to stay in the United States. It had been filled out six years after my father's birth, long after my grandmother had begun to have babies with another man. Francisco's date of birth is listed as October 27, 1916. Place of birth: Unknown. Hair: Black. Eyes: Brown. Height: Five feet, seven and a half inches. Nationality: Unknown. Race: White. The section for "Marks" reveals his hardscrabble life and rough profession: "broken nose; scar left nostril; scar under rt. eye, between eyebrows." Of interest to my father and me, the name and address of his nearest relative at home is "Wife: Eva Franklin Senna." He—or the person filling out the application—had gotten her name wrong. Once again an official document had rendered her nameless. From her nameless birth certificate to the mangled baptismal certificates of her children, names were paradoxically occasions for erasing the truth and the person. The document suggests that Francisco briefly married Anna in the forties in order to stay in the country, mistreated her, and abandoned her while she was pregnant. She returned to the South, to Father Ryan, desperate, and he introduced her to the family of Creoles in Jennings, Louisiana, the town where my father was born. The document too reveals that Francisco continued to use her long after they had parted ways. She became the name he used when he was trying to stay in the country. The truth was a sad and cruel reality, and yet my father was happy to have it—a confirmation of his father's existence—proof that she had at least in part told the truth about her marriage to a Mexican. Francisco's efforts to stay in the country were in vain. Across the form is stamped the word EXCLUDED.

Around the same time that my father discovered this record of his father's existence, he took a DNA test to find out the ethnic mix in his blood. He called me on my cell phone one afternoon with the results. I was at a playground with my son. My father sounded excited, pleased with what he'd found. The results of the DNA test claim to reveal "haplogroups . . . fractures in the family tree that are tied to deep ancestry." Legitimate or not, the test showed that my father had strong links to Native American Indian ancestry—the group most tied to the Mexican Indians. Later, when I got home, I received the e-mail he'd sent me and my siblings upon receiving the results: "Based on the Houston genetic research firm, Family Tree DNA Y Chromosome ancestral test, it looks like I am [Francisco José Senna's] kid . . . Of course, I could be another Mexican's kid, but with the ancestral chart putting me in with the Mongol line of Genghis Khan, the Spanish Conquistadors and the Mayas and Aztecs, it's all history. Past."

At the end of *Notes of a Native Son*, James Baldwin wrote: "This world is white no longer, and it will never be white again." It is black no longer too. And in reality, it was never simply black or white. When I look at the history of my mother's side, the DeWolfes, and trace it far enough back, it begins to collide with my father's history, and the two narratives become part of a shared story. My grandmother was an orphan. She found her only home in the Catholic Church, where she became mistress or lover, depending on whom you ask, to Father Ryan. The DeWolfe story is also a tale of orphans. During one of his slave-trading expeditions, my ancestor, Captain James DeWolf, captured two children in Africa and brought them back to Rhode Island as a "gift" for his wife:

> [The children] were captured at two different beaches on the same voyage of Captain Jim's brig, *Lavinia*: the girl when she was caught peering from behind a mangrove at the white men, and the boy while he was playing in the sand. They were of different tribes, he perhaps a Mandingo and she a Fula. On the

trip home the purser called them Pomp and Peggy. They became the pets of the voyage. When Nancy DeWolf received
them—they were a Christmas gift from her husband in 1803—
she gave them the more elegant names of Polydore and Agi-
way. When they came of age, she had them married in her
front parlor by Bishop Griswold. [from George Howe's *Mount
Hope*]

When he died in 1837, Captain DeWolf was the second-richest
man in the country. He owned the Mount, a "flamboyant" and
"imposing" old house in the slave port of Bristol, Rhode Island.

According to Helen Huntington Howe's *Gentle Americans*,
generations later my great-grandfather, Mark Anthony DeWolfe
Howe, the liberal historian of Beacon Hill, "gravely, sorrowfully,
and truthfully—if a trifle mutedly—recorded some of the appalling statistics of Bristol's slave trade . . . [He] tried to cheer
himself by the thought that he was not a direct lineal descendant of the nefarious Captain Jim."

But he did share blood with Captain Jim, and he shared a
family manse, and he even taught his own children to chant
a jolly rhyme learned during his own youth in Bristol:

> Agiway and Polydore
> Sitting on the cellar door;
> Polydore and Agiway,
> Sitting in the cellarway!
> Down fell the cellar door,
> Bump went Polydore;
> Up flew the cellarway,
> Off blew Agiway!

When I was growing up, my father often referred to his father as a Mexican Indian. He was proud of the Mayan Indian heritage he believed he carried in his blood. The DeWolfes' story is also a tale of Indians. The DeWolfes were descendants of the brigade that slaughtered one of the most notorious Indian warriors, Metacom of the Wampanoag tribe, who had nearly ended the English colonization of the Americas in a bloody battle of 1675. His chair—a rocky ledge where he set up his perch during the war—sits on the edge of Mount Hope in Bristol.

The different parts of my family, when I really look at them, seem not segregated at all, but rather interlocking pieces of the same incomplete puzzle.

My family is today, through blood and marriage, African American, Mexican, Polish Jew, Pakistani Muslim, Cuban, Chinese, Japanese, English, and Irish. We are wandering, spreading, splintering apart, all the time. We are trying to reinvent ourselves with each new generation. We are blending new races with each new union. I want to trace the origins of my multiracial family back to my grandmother, a slim, motherless black woman, who from the moment she was born was claimed by nobody.

This morning my son—fifteen months old—woke at four-thirty in the morning crying out in the nursery. I went and fed him a warm bottle of milk, and he ended up falling asleep on my lap, his little face tilted up toward mine, his full lips turned down at the corners as if he were listening to a complicated lecture in his dreams.

When he was heavily asleep, I stood up to put his sleeping body back in the crib—but he woke up and cried and clutched my nightgown, so I sat back down. In the end I held him there in the rocking chair for an hour and a half while he slept. I told myself it was because I wanted to make sure he got the rest, but really I was enjoying sitting in the dawn-dark room watching his face, so perfectly peaceful, as he slept. And when he finally awoke, it was as if he were drifting from one dream to another.

In the end perhaps it is our errors, our failures, even more than our triumphs, that make us who we are. Maybe it is the failed marriages and the failed revolutions—if we do survive them— that forge our character and core identity. The fetus grows, impervious to the circumstances that conceived it. The fetus grows, oblivious to the ambivalence and calamity that await its birth.

I am the product of a profound failure, a marriage so disastrous it looks in retrospect like a war. My brother, sister, and I were formed out of the biggest mistake of our parents' lives. For us, there is no before—no nostalgic moment of purity to harken back to, no motherland in Africa and Europe to shift our gaze away. There is only, always and already, the failure of this nation and of their union, from which we three emerge, bruised and battered but still breathing. This is our only homeland.

I end with a picture of them on their wedding night— Boston, October 27, 1968: a brown-skinned boy from the Roxbury housing projects by way of the Deep South, a blond, blue-eyed daughter of Cambridge intelligentsia about to carry her parents' liberal values to their most literal conclusion; the "negro of exceptional promise" taking the hand of the descendant of slave-traders. In the photograph they look both elated and weary from the celebration that has just ended. My mother is laughing, a cigarette in hand, and my father looks uneasy, his eyes averted. Together they will change the world through love, or some approximation of love. They hold hands, like two lost children out of a fairy tale, half-thrilled by their freedom, half afraid of it, as they wander deeper into the thickening center.

Acknowledgments

I am truly grateful to the New York Public Library's Cullman Center for Scholars and Writers for providing the space, time, and resources as I embarked on this project, with special thanks to Jean Strouse and Adriana Nova. My thanks to my editor, Jonathan Galassi, for his belief in this story, and for his encouragement, patience, and wisdom. Thank you to Gena Hamshaw, for her attentiveness, advice, and friendship throughout the process; to Wah-Ming Chang, for her special efforts on behalf of this book; and to my wonderful agent, Sarah Chalfant, for her help in shaping this idea and for finding a good home for it.

For those conversations, which directly and indirectly helped me through the process, thank you: Carol Munter, Jim Kincaid, Jennifer Egan, Farai Chideya, Maceo Senna, and my newfound aunts, Carla Latty and Crescentia "Sugar" Coutinho.

Thank you to Catholic Week and Catholic Charities for providing much needed materials.

I am ever grateful to Betty Jean Foy and Yvonne Jones, who welcomed me into their homes and were my guides on my trip to Alabama, offering me invaluable information about our family history. Thank you to Willie Maryland at the Alabama State

Acknowledgments

Archives, the late, great Odessa Redding, Dr. Norman C. Francis of Xavier University, and Xavier University of Louisiana archives.

Thank you to my husband who was at the other desk writing as I wrote this, and whose love and support sustained me as I struggled to tell this story.

To my father, who shared his life stories with me and included me in his own investigation into the truth of his origins, this story in so many ways belongs to you. Thank you for understanding—as one writer to another—that we all have our own truth to tell.